Homemade
AMISH
COOKING

Publications International, Ltd.

Art and photographs on front cover and pages 3 and 173 copyright © Shutterstock.com.

Pictured on the front cover *(top to bottom):* Honey Mustard Herbed Lamb with Vegetables *(page 50)* and Deep-Dish Blueberry Pie *(page 172)*.

Pictured on the back cover *(clockwise from top left):* Cranberry Pumpkin Nut Bread *(page 96)*, Raisin-Nut Oatmeal *(page 12)*, Garden Vegetable Soup *(page 58)*, Greens and Pears with Maple-Mustard Dressing *(page 78)*, Mashed Root Vegetables *(page 74)* and Old-Fashioned Chicken with Dumplings *(page 46)*.

ISBN: 978-1-64558-738-5

Manufactured in China.

8 7 6 5 4 3 2 1

WARNING: Food preparation, baking and cooking involve inherent dangers: misuse of electric products, sharp electric tools, boiling water, hot stoves, allergic reactions, foodborne illnesses and the like, pose numerous potential risks. Publications International, Ltd. (PIL) assumes no responsibility or liability for any damages you may experience as a result of following recipes, instructions, tips or advice in this publication.

While we hope this publication helps you find new ways to eat delicious foods, you may not always achieve the results desired due to variations in ingredients, cooking temperatures, typos, errors, omissions or individual cooking abilities.

Let's get social!
⊙ @Publications_International
f @PublicationsInternational
www.pilbooks.com

Table of Contents

CINNAMON SWIRL COFFEECAKE
Makes 9 to 12 servings

FILLING AND TOPPING

- 1/3 **cup all-purpose flour**
- 1/3 **cup granulated sugar**
- 1/3 **cup packed brown sugar**
- 1 1/2 **tablespoons ground cinnamon**
- 1/4 **teaspoon salt**
- 1/8 **teaspoon ground allspice**
- 3 **tablespoons melted butter**

CAKE

- 2 **cups all-purpose flour**
- 1 1/2 **teaspoons baking powder**
- 3/4 **teaspoon baking soda**
- 1/2 **teaspoon salt**
- 9 **tablespoons butter, softened**
- 1 1/4 **cups granulated sugar**
- 3 **eggs**
- 1/2 **cup sour cream**
- 2 **teaspoons vanilla**
- 3/4 **cup milk**

1. Preheat oven to 350°F. Grease 9-inch square baking pan.

2. For filling, combine 1/3 cup flour, 1/3 cup granulated sugar, brown sugar, cinnamon, 1/4 teaspoon salt and allspice in small bowl; mix well. For topping, remove half of mixture to another small bowl; stir in melted butter until blended.

3. For cake, combine 2 cups flour, baking powder, baking soda and 1/2 teaspoon salt in medium bowl; mix well. Combine 9 tablespoons butter and 1 1/4 cups granulated sugar in large bowl; beat with electric mixer at medium speed 3 minutes or until light and fluffy. Add eggs, sour cream and vanilla; beat until well blended. Scrape down side of bowl. Add flour mixture alternately with milk in two additions, beating at low speed until blended. Spread half of batter in prepared pan; sprinkle evenly with filling. Spread remaining batter over filling with dampened hands. Sprinkle with topping.

4. Bake 45 to 50 minutes or until toothpick inserted into center comes out clean. Cool completely in pan on wire rack.

ZUCCHINI BREAD PANCAKES

Makes 6 pancakes

1 medium zucchini, grated

¼ cup plain yogurt

1 egg

2 tablespoons milk

3 tablespoons vegetable oil, divided

½ cup whole wheat flour

2 tablespoons packed brown sugar

1 teaspoon grated lemon peel, plus additional for garnish

1 teaspoon baking soda

½ teaspoon salt

½ teaspoon ground cinnamon

⅛ teaspoon ground nutmeg

Maple syrup

1. Combine zucchini, yogurt, egg, milk and 1 tablespoon oil in large bowl; mix well. Add flour, brown sugar, 1 teaspoon lemon peel, baking soda, salt, cinnamon and nutmeg; stir just until combined.

2. Heat 1 tablespoon oil in large griddle or skillet over medium-low heat. Pour ¼ cupfuls of batter 2 inches apart onto griddle. Cook 3 minutes or until lightly browned and edges begin to bubble. Turn over; cook 3 minutes or until lightly browned. Repeat with remaining 1 tablespoon oil and batter.

3. Serve with maple syrup and garnish with additional lemon peel.

Hearty Breakfasts

HAM AND CHEESE BREAD PUDDING

Makes 8 servings

- 1 **small loaf (8 ounces) sourdough, country French or Italian bread, sliced**
- 3 **tablespoons butter, softened**
- 8 **ounces ham or smoked ham, cubed**
- 1 **cup (4 ounces) shredded Cheddar cheese**
- 3 **eggs**
- 2 **cups milk**
- 1 **teaspoon ground mustard**
- ½ **teaspoon salt**
- ⅛ **teaspoon white pepper**

1. Grease 11×7-inch baking dish. Spread one side of each bread slice with butter. Cut into 1-inch cubes; place on bottom of prepared baking dish. Top with ham; sprinkle with cheese.

2. Beat eggs in medium bowl. Whisk in milk, mustard, salt and pepper until blended. Pour egg mixture evenly over bread mixture; cover and refrigerate at least 6 hours or overnight.

3. Preheat oven to 350°F. Bake bread pudding, uncovered, 45 to 50 minutes or until puffed and golden brown and knife inserted into center comes out clean. Serve immediately.

Hearty Breakfasts

OAT CAKES WITH RASPBERRY TOPPING

Makes 6 servings

1 pint raspberries, divided

8 tablespoons sugar, divided

2 tablespoons cornstarch

½ cup water

1 teaspoon lemon juice

½ cup quick oats

1 cup whole wheat flour

2½ teaspoons baking powder

½ teaspoon salt

1¼ cups milk

½ cup plain yogurt

1 tablespoon vegetable oil

1. Place half of raspberries in medium bowl; mash with potato masher.

2. Combine 5 tablespoons sugar and cornstarch in small saucepan. Stir in water until smooth. Cook and stir over medium heat until mixture comes to a boil. Add lemon juice and mashed raspberries; return to a boil. Remove from heat; let stand 15 minutes. Stir in remaining whole raspberries.

3. Place oats in small skillet; cook and stir over medium heat 3 minutes or until lightly browned. Place in medium bowl; cool completely.

4. Stir in flour, baking powder, salt and remaining 3 tablespoons sugar. Combine milk and yogurt in small bowl; stir into flour mixture just until dry ingredients are moistened. (Batter will be lumpy.)

5. Heat oil in large skillet over medium heat until water droplets sprinkled on skillet bounce off surface. Drop batter by scant ¼ cupfuls onto griddle; spread batter to form 4-inch round cakes. Cook 2 minutes or until top is covered with bubbles. Turn cakes; cook 2 minutes longer or until browned. Repeat with remaining batter, adding additional oil if needed. Serve warm with raspberry topping.

VARIATION: Blueberries or sliced hulled strawberries can be substituted for the raspberries. Mash half the berries and leave the rest whole.

Hearty Breakfasts

RAISIN-NUT OATMEAL
Makes 4 servings

2³/₄ cups water

1 cup milk

2²/₃ cups old-fashioned oats

²/₃ cup raisins

¹/₃ cup packed brown sugar

¹/₂ teaspoon salt

¹/₂ teaspoon ground cinnamon

¹/₈ teaspoon ground ginger

¹/₂ cup sliced almonds, toasted*

*To toast almonds, cook in medium skillet over medium heat 3 to 4 minutes or until lightly browned and fragrant, stirring frequently.

1. Bring water and milk to a boil in large saucepan over high heat. Stir in oats, raisins, brown sugar, salt, cinnamon and ginger.

2. Reduce heat to medium. Cook and stir 4 to 5 minutes or until thick and creamy. Stir in almonds.

Hearty Breakfasts

SUGAR AND SPICE DOUGHNUTS
Makes 14 to 16 doughnuts

2³/₄ **cups all-purpose flour**

¹/₄ **cup cornstarch**

1 **teaspoon salt**

1 **teaspoon baking powder**

¹/₂ **teaspoon baking soda**

¹/₂ **teaspoon ground cinnamon**

¹/₂ **teaspoon ground nutmeg**

1 **cup sugar**

2 **eggs**

¹/₄ **cup (¹/₂ stick) butter,
    melted**

¹/₄ **cup applesauce**

1 **teaspoon vanilla**

¹/₂ **cup buttermilk**

Vegetable oil for frying

TOPPING

1 **cup sugar**

1 **teaspoon ground cinnamon**

1. Whisk flour, cornstarch, salt, baking powder, baking soda, ¹/₂ teaspoon cinnamon and nutmeg in large bowl.

2. Beat 1 cup sugar and eggs in large bowl with electric mixer on high speed 3 minutes or until pale and thick. Stir in butter, applesauce and vanilla. Add flour mixture alternately with buttermilk, mixing on low speed after each addition. Press plastic wrap directly onto surface of dough; refrigerate at least 1 hour.

3. Pour about 2 inches of oil into Dutch oven or large heavy saucepan; clip deep-fry or candy thermometer to side of pot. Heat over medium-high heat to 360° to 370°F.

4. Meanwhile, generously flour work surface. Turn out dough onto work surface and dust top with flour (dough will be sticky). Roll dough about ¹/₄-inch thick; cut out doughnuts with floured doughnut cutter. Gather and reroll scraps. For topping, combine 1 cup sugar and 1 teaspoon cinnamon in large bowl. Line large wire rack with paper towels.

5. Working in batches, add doughnuts to hot oil. Cook 1 minute per side or until golden brown. Do not crowd the pan and adjust heat to maintain temperature during frying. Drain doughnuts briefly on prepared wire rack, then toss in topping to coat both sides. Cool on wire racks. If desired, fry doughnut holes 1 minute. Drain; toss in topping to coat.

Hearty Breakfasts

TIP: The oil for frying can be reused for several batches of doughnuts. When the oil is completely cool, strain it through a fine-mesh strainer into a jar or container with tight-fitting lid and store it in the refrigerator. When you make your next batch of doughnuts, add additional fresh oil to it to fill the pot about 2 inches deep. Use the oil up to three times and then start over with new oil.

CLASSIC CINNAMON BUNS
Makes 12 buns

DOUGH

- **1 package (¼ ounce) instant or rapid-rise active dry yeast**
- **1 cup warm milk (110°F)**
- **2 eggs, beaten**
- **½ cup granulated sugar**
- **¼ cup (½ stick) butter, softened**
- **1 teaspoon salt**
- **4 to 4¼ cups all-purpose flour**

FILLING

- **1 cup packed brown sugar**
- **3 tablespoons ground cinnamon**
- **Pinch salt**
- **6 tablespoons (¾ stick) butter, softened**

ICING

- **1½ cups powdered sugar**
- **3 ounces cream cheese, softened**
- **¼ cup (½ stick) butter, softened**
- **½ teaspoon vanilla**
- **⅛ teaspoon salt**

1. Dissolve yeast in warm milk in large bowl of electric stand mixer. Add eggs, granulated sugar, ¼ cup butter and 1 teaspoon salt; beat at medium speed until well blended. Add 4 cups flour; beat at low speed until dough begins to come together. Knead dough with dough hook at low speed about 5 minutes or until dough is smooth, elastic and slightly sticky. Add additional flour, 1 tablespoon at a time, if necessary to prevent sticking.

2. Shape dough into a ball. Place in large greased bowl; turn to grease top. Cover and let rise in warm place about 1 hour or until doubled in size. Meanwhile, for filling, combine brown sugar, cinnamon and pinch of salt in small bowl; mix well.

3. Grease 13×9-inch baking pan. Roll out dough into 18×14-inch rectangle on floured surface. Spread 6 tablespoons butter evenly over dough; top with cinnamon-sugar mixture. Beginning with long side, roll up dough tightly jelly-roll style; pinch seam to seal. Cut log crosswise into 12 slices; place slices cut sides up in prepared pan. Cover and let rise in warm place about 30 minutes or until rolls are touching and have almost doubled in size. Preheat oven to 350°F.

4. Bake 20 to 25 minutes or until golden brown. Meanwhile for icing, combine powdered sugar, cream cheese, ¼ cup butter, vanilla and ⅛ teaspoon salt in medium bowl; beat with electric mixer at medium speed 2 minutes or until smooth and creamy. Spread icing over warm cinnamon buns.

SAUSAGE AND APPLE QUICHE
Makes 6 servings

Single-Crust Pie Pastry (page 162)

½ **pound bulk spicy pork sausage**

½ **cup chopped onion**

¾ **cup shredded peeled tart apple**

1 **tablespoon lemon juice**

1 **tablespoon sugar**

⅛ **teaspoon red pepper flakes**

1 **cup (4 ounces) shredded Cheddar cheese**

1½ **cups half-and-half**

3 **eggs**

¼ **teaspoon salt**

Dash black pepper

1. Prepare pie pastry. Roll out into 11-inch circle on lightly floured surface. Line 9-inch pie plate with pastry; trim and flute edge. Refrigerate until ready to fill.

2. Preheat oven to 450°F. Line crust with foil; partially fill with uncooked beans or rice. Bake 10 minutes. Remove foil and beans; bake crust 5 minutes or until lightly browned. Let cool. *Reduce oven temperature to 375°F.*

3. Crumble sausage into large skillet; add onion. Cook and stir over medium heat until sausage is browned and onion is tender. Spoon off and discard pan drippings. Add apple, lemon juice, sugar and red pepper flakes; cook and stir 4 minutes or until apple is barely tender and all liquid is evaporated. Let cool slightly. Spoon sausage mixture into crust; sprinkle with cheese.

4. Whisk half-and-half, eggs and salt in medium bowl; season with black pepper. Pour over sausage mixture in crust.

5. Bake 35 to 45 minutes or until filling is puffed and knife inserted into center comes out clean. Let stand 10 minutes before serving.

Hearty Breakfasts

CRULLERS
Makes about 12 doughnuts

Vegetable oil for frying

1 cup water

½ cup (1 stick) butter, cut into ¼-inch pieces

1 cup all-purpose flour

½ teaspoon salt

3 eggs

GLAZE

2 tablespoons butter

1 cup powdered sugar

1 tablespoon milk or cream

1 teaspoon vanilla

1. Pour about 2 inches of oil into Dutch oven or large heavy saucepan; clip deep-fry or candy thermometer to side of pot. Heat over medium-high heat to 350° to 360°F. Line large wire rack with paper towels.

2. Meanwhile, bring water and ½ cup butter to a boil in medium saucepan over high heat; stir until butter melts. Add flour and salt all at once, stirring vigorously. Continue cooking and stirring until mixture forms ball and pulls away from side of pan. Remove from heat. Add eggs, one at a time, beating vigorously after each addition until mixture is smooth.

3. Transfer dough to large piping bag fitted with large star tip (fill bag half full and replenish as needed). Pipe 3-inch circles onto greased baking sheet.

4. Working in batches, add doughnuts to hot oil. Cook 2 minutes per side or until golden brown. Do not crowd the pan and adjust heat to maintain temperature during frying. Drain doughnuts on prepared wire rack.

5. For glaze, melt 2 tablespoons butter in small saucepan over low heat. Whisk in powdered sugar and milk; cook 1 minute or until mixture is smooth. Whisk in vanilla. Working quickly, dip tops of doughnuts into glaze; place on wire rack. If glaze hardens, rewarm briefly over low heat.

Hearty Breakfasts

HAM AND SPINACH PUFF PIE

Makes 4 to 6 servings

- **2 cups (about 1 pound) diced cooked ham**
- **1 package (10 ounces) frozen chopped spinach, thawed and squeezed dry**
- **1/2 cup diced red bell pepper**
- **4 green onions, sliced**
- **3 eggs**
- **3/4 cup all-purpose flour**
- **3/4 cup (3 ounces) shredded Swiss cheese**
- **3/4 cup milk**
- **1 tablespoon Dijon or whole-grain mustard**
- **1 teaspoon grated lemon peel**
- **1 teaspoon dried dill weed**
- **1/2 teaspoon garlic salt**
- **1/2 teaspoon black pepper**

1. Preheat oven to 425°F. Grease 2-quart round baking dish.

2. Combine ham, spinach, bell pepper and green onions in prepared baking dish. Beat eggs in medium bowl. Stir in flour, cheese, milk, mustard, lemon peel, dill weed, garlic salt and black pepper; mix well. Pour over ham mixture.

3. Bake 30 to 35 minutes or until puffed and browned. Cut into wedges.

Hearty Breakfasts

GERMAN APPLE PANCAKE
Makes 6 servings

1 tablespoon butter

1 large *or* 2 small apples, peeled and thinly sliced (about 1½ cups)

1 tablespoon packed brown sugar

1½ teaspoons ground cinnamon, divided

2 eggs

2 egg whites

1 tablespoon granulated sugar

1 teaspoon vanilla

¼ teaspoon salt

½ cup all-purpose flour

½ cup milk

Maple syrup (optional)

1. Preheat oven to 425°F.

2. Melt butter in medium cast iron or ovenproof skillet over medium heat. Add apples, brown sugar and ½ teaspoon cinnamon; cook and stir 5 minutes or until apples just begin to soften. Remove from heat. Arrange apple slices in single layer in skillet.

3. Whisk eggs, egg whites, granulated sugar, remaining 1 teaspoon cinnamon, vanilla and salt in medium bowl until well blended. Stir in flour and milk until smooth and well blended. Pour evenly over apples.

4. Bake 20 to 25 minutes or until puffed and golden brown. Serve with maple syrup, if desired.

NOTE: Pancake will fall slightly after being removed from the oven.

FAMILY DINNERS

SIMPLE ROASTED CHICKEN
Makes 4 servings

1 whole chicken (about 4 pounds)

3 tablespoons butter, softened

1½ teaspoons salt

1 teaspoon onion powder

1 teaspoon dried thyme

½ teaspoon garlic powder

½ teaspoon paprika

½ teaspoon black pepper

Fresh parsley sprigs and lemon wedges (optional)

1. Preheat oven to 425°F. Pat chicken dry; place in small baking dish or on baking sheet.

2. Combine butter, salt, onion powder, thyme, garlic powder, paprika and pepper in small bowl; mash with fork until well blended. Loosen skin on breasts and thighs; spread about one third of butter mixture under skin.

3. Melt remaining butter mixture; brush all over outside of chicken and inside cavity. Tie drumsticks together with kitchen string and tuck wing tips under.

4. Roast 20 minutes. *Reduce oven temperature to 375°F.* Roast 45 to 55 minutes or until chicken is cooked through (165°F), basting once with pan juices during last 10 minutes of cooking time.

5. Remove chicken to cutting board; tent with foil. Let stand at least 15 minutes before carving. Garnish with parsley and lemon wedges.

BEEF AND PEPPER CASSEROLE WITH NOODLES

Makes 4 servings

1 pound ground beef

1 cup chopped green bell pepper

1 cup chopped yellow onion

1 can (8 ounces) tomato sauce with basil, garlic and oregano

2 teaspoons Worcestershire sauce

½ teaspoon salt

8 ounces uncooked egg noodles

¼ cup chopped fresh parsley

1. Heat large skillet over medium-high heat. Add beef; cook and stir 6 to 8 minutes or until no longer pink, stirring to break up beef with wooden spoon. Drain and transfer beef to bowl.

2. Add bell pepper and onion to same skillet; cook and stir over medium-high heat 5 minutes or until onion is translucent. Return beef to skillet. Add tomato sauce, Worcestershire sauce and salt; stir to blend. Bring to a boil. Reduce heat; cover and simmer 15 minutes or until onion is tender.

3. Meanwhile, cook pasta in large saucepan of salted boiling water according to package directions for al dente. Drain and return to saucepan.

4. Remove meat mixture from heat. Cover and let stand 5 minutes. Serve beef mixture over cooked pasta. Sprinkle with parsley.

SLOW COOKED PORK AND SAUERKRAUT

Makes 6 servings

- 2 jars (32 ounces each) sauerkraut, rinsed and drained
- 2½ cups water
- 3 tablespoons brown mustard
- 1 package (1 ounce) dry onion soup mix
- 3 pounds boneless pork loin roast

SLOW COOKER DIRECTIONS

1. Combine sauerkraut, water, mustard and soup mix in slow cooker; mix well. Add pork to slow cooker.

2. Cover; cook on LOW 8 hours. Slice pork; serve with sauerkraut.

Family Dinners

SUNDAY DINNER CASSEROLE
Makes 4 to 6 servings

2 **cups egg noodles, cooked and drained**

2 **pounds boneless skinless chicken breasts, pounded ½-inch thick if large**

2 **cups sliced sweet onions**

½ **cup dry sherry**

2 **tablespoons sugar**

2 **tablespoons balsamic vinegar**

1 **teaspoon dried thyme**

½ **teaspoon salt**

½ **teaspoon black pepper**

3 **cups chicken broth**

1 **can (about 14 ounces) diced tomatoes**

2 **cloves garlic, minced**

½ **teaspoon red pepper flakes**

¼ **cup chopped fresh basil**

2 **teaspoons grated lemon peel**

1. Preheat oven to 400°F. Place noodles in 13×9-inch baking dish. Top with chicken.

2. Meanwhile, combine onions, sherry, sugar, vinegar, thyme, salt and black pepper in large skillet. Cook and stir over medium heat about 15 minutes or until onions begin to brown. Add broth, tomatoes, garlic and red pepper flakes to onion mixture in skillet. Pour over chicken.

3. Bake 20 minutes. Turn chicken; bake 20 to 25 minutes or until chicken is no longer pink in center. Sprinkle with basil and lemon peel.

OLD-FASHIONED CABBAGE ROLLS

Makes 8 servings

8 ounces ground beef

8 ounces ground veal

8 ounces ground pork

1 small onion, chopped

2 eggs

½ cup plain dry bread crumbs

1 teaspoon salt

1 teaspoon molasses

¼ teaspoon ground ginger

¼ teaspoon ground nutmeg

¼ teaspoon ground allspice

1 large head cabbage, separated into leaves

3 cups boiling water

¼ cup (½ stick) butter

½ cup milk, plus additional if necessary

1 tablespoon cornstarch

1. Combine beef, veal, pork and onion in large bowl. Combine eggs, bread crumbs, salt, molasses, ginger, nutmeg and allspice in medium bowl; mix well. Add to meat mixture; stir until well blended.

2. Drop cabbage leaves into boiling water; cook 3 minutes. Remove with slotted spoon; reserve ½ cup boiling liquid.

3. Preheat oven to 375°F. Place about 2 tablespoons meat mixture about 1 inch from stem end of each cabbage leaf. Fold sides in and roll up, fastening with toothpicks, if necessary.

4. Heat butter in large skillet over medium-high heat. Add cabbage rolls, 3 or 4 at a time; brown on all sides. Arrange rolls, seam side down, in single layer in large baking dish. Combine reserved boiling liquid with butter remaining in skillet; pour over cabbage rolls.

5. Bake 1 hour. Carefully drain accumulated pan juices into measuring cup. Return cabbage rolls to oven.

6. Add enough milk to pan juices to equal 1 cup. Pour milk mixture into small saucepan. Stir in cornstarch; bring to a boil, stirring constantly until sauce is thickened. Pour over cabbage rolls. Bake 15 minutes or until cabbage is tender and sauce is bubbly.

BEEF POT PIE WITH CHEDDAR BISCUITS

Makes 6 servings

6 tablespoons all-purpose flour

¾ teaspoon celery salt, divided

¼ teaspoon black pepper, divided

2 pounds cubed beef stew meat

4 to 5 tablespoons vegetable oil, divided

1½ cups beef broth

½ teaspoon dried thyme

1 cup pearl onions (12 to 15)

1½ cups cubed red potatoes

1 cup sliced carrots (quartered lengthwise and cut crosswise into thirds)

1 cup cut green beans (1-inch pieces)

Cheddar Biscuits (page 37)

1. Combine flour, ¼ teaspoon celery salt and ⅛ teaspoon pepper in large resealable food storage bag; shake until blended. Place one third of beef cubes in bag; seal. Shake until beef is coated. Shake off excess flour mixture.

2. Heat 2 tablespoons oil in Dutch oven over medium heat. Add beef; cook until lightly browned on all sides. Transfer beef to bowl. Repeat with remaining beef and flour mixture, adding additional 2 tablespoons oil if needed. Reserve remaining flour mixture.

3. Add remaining 1 tablespoon oil and 2 tablespoons reserved flour mixture to Dutch oven; cook and stir 1 minute. Gradually add broth, stirring to scrape up browned bits. Return beef to Dutch oven. Stir in thyme, remaining ½ teaspoon celery salt and ⅛ teaspoon pepper. Reduce heat to medium-low; cover and simmer 45 minutes.

4. Meanwhile, bring 2 cups water to a boil in small saucepan. Add onions; boil 30 seconds. Drain and rinse under cold water until cool enough to handle. Remove root ends of onions; peel.

5. Add onions, potatoes and carrots to beef mixture. Cover and cook 20 to 25 minutes or until beef is tender.

6. Preheat oven to 425°F. Grease 2½-quart baking dish. Add green beans and additional broth to Dutch oven if gravy is too thick. Simmer 5 minutes. Transfer to prepared baking dish.

7. Prepare Cheddar Biscuits. Arrange biscuits on top of beef mixture. Bake 12 to 15 minutes or until biscuits are golden brown.

CHEDDAR BISCUITS

1½ **cups all-purpose flour**

1½ **teaspoons baking powder**

½ **teaspoon salt**

¼ **teaspoon baking soda**

¼ **cup (½ stick) cold butter, cut into ¼-inch pieces**

½ **cup (2 ounces) shredded Cheddar cheese**

2 **tablespoons snipped fresh chives**

⅔ **cup buttermilk**

1. Combine flour, baking powder, salt and baking soda in medium bowl. Cut in butter with pastry blender or fingertips until mixture resembles coarse crumbs. Stir in cheese and chives. Add buttermilk; stir until soft dough forms.

2. Knead dough four times on floured surface. Pat dough into ½-inch-thick circle. Cut out biscuits with 2-inch round cutter. Gather scraps and pat ½-inch thick; cut additional biscuits.

NOTE: To bake biscuits to serve with other dishes, arrange them on a baking sheet and bake at 450°F for 10 to 12 minutes or until tops are browned.

SAUERBRATEN WITH GINGER GRAVY

Makes 6 to 8 servings

3 cups water

1 cup cider vinegar

1 onion, thinly sliced

3 tablespoons packed brown sugar

2 cloves garlic, crushed

1½ teaspoons salt

1 teaspoon ground ginger

1 teaspoon whole allspice

1 teaspoon whole cloves

½ teaspoon juniper berries

1 beef rump roast (about 4 pounds)

2 tablespoons vegetable oil

2 tablespoons all-purpose flour

¼ cup crushed gingersnap cookies

1. For marinade, bring water and vinegar to a boil in large saucepan over high heat. Remove from heat; add onion, brown sugar, garlic, salt, ginger, allspice, cloves and juniper berries. Cool slightly.

2. Place roast in large glass bowl or large resealable food storage bag; pour marinade over roast. Cover bowl or seal bag; marinate in refrigerator at least 8 hours, turning occasionally.

3. Remove roast from marinade, reserving marinade. Pat roast dry with paper towels. Heat oil in Dutch oven over medium-high heat. Add roast; brown on all sides. Add marinade to Dutch oven. Reduce heat to low; cover and cook 2½ to 3 hours or until fork-tender. Remove roast from Dutch oven; set aside.

4. Strain braising liquid through fine-mesh sieve into large bowl; discard spices and onion. Skim fat from braising liquid; discard. Measure 2 cups liquid; discard remaining liquid. Place 1½ cups liquid in Dutch oven. Place flour in small bowl; gradually whisk remaining ½ cup liquid into flour. Stir mixture into liquid in Dutch oven. Add gingersnaps; mix well. Bring to a boil over medium-high heat.

5. Return roast to Dutch oven. Reduce heat to low; cover and cook 15 to 20 minutes until flavors blend and sauce thickens. Slice roast and serve with sauce.

BEEF GOULASH

Makes 8 servings

¼ cup all-purpose flour

1 tablespoon Hungarian sweet paprika

1½ teaspoons salt

½ teaspoon Hungarian hot paprika

½ teaspoon black pepper

2 pounds cubed beef stew meat

4 tablespoons vegetable oil, divided

1 large onion, chopped

4 cloves garlic, minced

2 cans (about 14 ounces each) beef broth

1 can (about 14 ounces) stewed tomatoes

1 cup water

1 tablespoon dried marjoram

1 green bell pepper, chopped

3 cups uncooked thin egg noodles

Sour cream

1. Combine flour, sweet paprika, salt, hot paprika and black pepper in large resealable food storage bag. Add half of beef. Seal bag; shake to coat well.

2. Heat 1½ tablespoons oil in Dutch oven over medium heat. Add half of beef; brown on all sides. Transfer to large bowl. Repeat with remaining flour mixture, beef and 1½ tablespoons oil; transfer to same bowl.

3. Heat remaining 1 tablespoon oil in same Dutch oven. Add onion and garlic; cook and stir 5 minutes or until tender.

4. Return beef and any accumulated juices to Dutch oven. Add broth, tomatoes, water and marjoram. Bring to a boil over medium-high heat. Reduce heat; cover and simmer 1½ hours or until meat is tender, stirring once.

5. Stir in bell pepper and noodles. Cover and simmer about 8 minutes or until noodles are tender, stirring once. Ladle into bowls; top with sour cream.

Family Dinners

CHICKEN POT PIE

Makes 4 servings

1½ pounds bone-in chicken pieces

1 cup chicken broth

½ teaspoon salt

¼ teaspoon black pepper

Single-Crust Pie Pastry (page 162)

1 to 1½ cups milk

3 tablespoons butter

1 medium onion, chopped

1 cup sliced celery

⅓ cup all-purpose flour

2 cups mixed vegetables (broccoli and/or cauliflower florets, sliced carrots, peas, chopped bell pepper)

1 tablespoon chopped fresh parsley *or* 1 teaspoon dried parsley flakes

½ teaspoon dried thyme

1 egg, lightly beaten

1. Combine chicken, broth, salt and pepper in large saucepan over medium-high heat; bring to a boil. Reduce heat to low; cover and simmer 30 minutes or until chicken is cooked through (165°F).

2. Meanwhile, prepare pie pastry.

3. Remove chicken from saucepan and let cool. Pour remaining chicken broth mixture into 4-cup glass measure. Add enough milk to broth mixture to equal 2½ cups. Remove chicken from bones and cut into ½-inch pieces.

4. Preheat oven to 400°F. Melt butter in same saucepan over medium heat. Add onion and celery; cook and stir 3 minutes or until tender. Stir in flour until well blended. Gradually stir in broth mixture. Cook until sauce boils and thickens, stirring constantly. Add chicken, vegetables, parsley and thyme. Pour into 1½-quart round baking dish.

5. Roll out pie pastry to 1 inch larger than diameter of baking dish on lightly floured surface. Cut slits in crust to vent; place on top of casserole. Trim and flute edge. If desired, reroll scraps and cut into decorative shapes; place on crust. Brush with beaten egg. Bake 30 minutes or until crust is golden brown and filling is bubbly.

Family Dinners

SALMON AND NOODLE CASSEROLE

Makes 4 servings

- **6 ounces uncooked wide egg noodles**
- **1 teaspoon vegetable oil**
- **1 onion, finely chopped**
- **³/₄ cup thinly sliced carrot**
- **³/₄ cup thinly sliced celery**
- **1 can (about 15 ounces) salmon, drained, skin and bones discarded**
- **1 can (10³/₄ ounces) condensed cream of celery soup, undiluted**
- **1 cup (4 ounces) shredded Cheddar cheese**
- **³/₄ cup frozen peas**
- **¹/₂ cup sour cream**
- **¹/₄ cup milk**
- **2 teaspoons dried dill weed**
- **Black pepper**
- **Chopped fresh dill (optional)**

1. Preheat oven to 350°F.

2. Cook noodles in large saucepan of salted boiling water according to package directions for al dente. Drain and return to saucepan.

3. Heat oil in large skillet over medium heat. Add onion, carrot and celery; cook and stir 5 minutes or until carrot is crisp-tender. Add to noodles with salmon, soup, cheese, peas, sour cream, milk, dill weed and pepper; stir gently to coat. Pour into 2-quart baking dish.

4. Cover and bake 25 minutes or until hot and bubbly. Garnish with fresh dill.

OLD-FASHIONED CHICKEN WITH DUMPLINGS

Makes 6 servings

STEW

- 3 tablespoons butter
- 3 to 3½ pounds bone-in chicken pieces
- 3 cans (about 14 ounces each) chicken broth
- 3½ cups water
- 1 teaspoon salt
- ½ teaspoon dried rosemary
- ¼ teaspoon white pepper
- 2 large carrots, cut into 1-inch slices
- 2 stalks celery, cut into 1-inch slices
- 8 to 10 pearl onions, peeled
- 8 ounces small mushrooms, cut into halves
- ½ cup frozen peas

DUMPLINGS

- 2 cups all-purpose flour
- 4 teaspoons baking powder
- 1 teaspoon salt
- 5 tablespoons cold butter, cut into ¼-pieces
- 1 cup milk
- 2 tablespoons chopped fresh parsley

1. Melt 3 tablespoons butter in large Dutch oven over medium-high heat. Add chicken; cook until golden brown on all sides.

2. Add broth, water, 1 teaspoon salt, rosemary and pepper; bring to a boil over high heat. Reduce heat to low; cover and simmer 15 minutes. Add carrots, celery, onions and mushrooms; cover and simmer 40 minutes or until chicken and vegetables are tender.

3. For dumplings, whisk flour, baking powder and 1 teaspoon salt in medium bowl. Cut in 5 tablespoons butter with pastry blender or fingertips until mixture resembles coarse crumbs. Make well in center; pour in milk. Add parsley; stir with fork until mixture forms ball.

4. When chicken is tender, skim fat from broth. Stir in peas. Drop dumpling mixture into broth, making 12 dumplings. Cover and simmer 15 to 20 minutes or until dumplings are firm and toothpick inserted into centers comes out clean.

BROWNED PORK CHOPS
WITH GRAVY

Makes 4 servings

½ **teaspoon dried sage**

½ **teaspoon dried marjoram**

¼ **teaspoon salt**

¼ **teaspoon black pepper**

4 **boneless pork loin chops (about 1 pound)**

1 **tablespoon vegetable oil**

¼ **cup chopped onion**

1 **clove garlic, minced**

1 **cup sliced mushrooms**

¾ **cup beef broth**

⅓ **cup sour cream**

1 **tablespoon all-purpose flour**

1 **teaspoon Dijon mustard**

2 **cups hot cooked wide egg noodles**

Chopped fresh parsley (optional)

1. Combine sage, marjoram, salt and pepper in small bowl. Rub onto both sides of chops.

2. Heat oil in large skillet over medium heat. Add chops; cook 5 minutes or until barely pink in center, turning once. Transfer to plate; keep warm.

3. Add onion and garlic to same skillet; cook and stir 2 minutes. Add mushrooms and broth; bring to a boil. Reduce heat to medium-low; cover and simmer 3 to 4 minutes or until mushrooms are tender.

4. Whisk sour cream, flour and mustard in medium bowl. Whisk in about 3 tablespoons broth mixture from skillet. Stir sour cream mixture into skillet. Cook and stir until mixture is hot and thickened. Serve gravy over pork chops and noodles. Garnish with parsley.

HONEY MUSTARD HERBED LAMB WITH VEGETABLES

Makes 4 servings

3 **tablespoons finely chopped fresh parsley**

2 **tablespoons minced fresh rosemary**

2 **cloves garlic, minced**

1¼ **teaspoons salt**

½ **teaspoon black pepper**

¼ **cup olive oil**

2 **tablespoons honey**

2 **tablespoons whole grain mustard**

4 **lamb shoulder chops (6 to 8 ounces each)**

1 **pound unpeeled small red potatoes, cut into halves (or quarters if large)**

1 **pound unpeeled small yellow potatoes, cut into halves (or quarters if large)**

1½ **pounds medium carrots, peeled, cut in half lengthwise then cut into 2-inch lengths**

1. Preheat oven to 425°F. Combine parsley, rosemary, garlic, salt and pepper in small bowl; mix well. Stir in oil until well blended.

2. Remove half of mixture to large shallow dish; stir in honey and mustard. Add lamb chops to dish; turn to coat both sides with mustard mixture. Set aside to marinate while preparing vegetables.

3. Combine potatoes and carrots on baking sheet. Stir remaining half of oil mixture; drizzle over vegetables and toss to coat. Cover baking sheet with foil.

4. Roast 40 minutes. Uncover; stir vegetables and roast 10 minutes. Remove baking sheet from oven; *turn oven to broil.* Arrange lamb chops over vegetables.

5. Broil 6 minutes. Turn lamb; broil 6 minutes or until medium (140°F). (Cooking time may vary depending on how quickly oven reaches broiling temperature.)

Family Dinners

CRISPY BUTTERMILK FRIED CHICKEN

Makes 4 servings

- **2 cups buttermilk**
- **1 tablespoon hot pepper sauce**
- **3 pounds bone-in chicken pieces**
- **2 cups all-purpose flour**
- **2 teaspoons salt**
- **2 teaspoons poultry seasoning**
- **1 teaspoon garlic salt**
- **1 teaspoon paprika**
- **1 teaspoon ground red pepper**
- **1 teaspoon black pepper**
- **1 cup vegetable oil**

1. Combine buttermilk and hot pepper sauce in large resealable food storage bag. Add chicken; seal bag. Turn to coat. Refrigerate 2 hours or up to 24 hours.

2. Combine flour, salt, poultry seasoning, garlic salt, paprika, red pepper and black pepper in another large resealable food storage bag or shallow baking dish; mix well. Working in batches, remove chicken from buttermilk; let excess drip back into bowl. Add to flour mixture; shake to coat.

3. Heat oil in heavy deep skillet over medium heat until deep-fry thermometer registers 350°F. Working in batches, fry chicken 30 minutes or until cooked through (165°F), turning occasionally to brown all sides. Drain on paper towels.

NOTE: Carefully monitor the temperature of the oil during cooking. It should not drop below 325°F or go higher than 350°F. Keep cooked chicken warm in 200°F oven on a wire rack on a baking sheet while the remaining chicken is cooking.

SAUERKRAUT PORK RIBS
Makes 12 servings

1 tablespoon vegetable oil

3 to 4 pounds country-style pork ribs

1 large onion, thinly sliced

1 teaspoon caraway seeds

½ teaspoon salt

½ teaspoon garlic powder

¼ to ½ teaspoon black pepper

¾ cup water

1 jar (about 28 ounces) sauerkraut

6 medium red potatoes, quartered

SLOW COOKER DIRECTIONS

1. Heat oil in large skillet over medium heat. Cook ribs in batches, turning to brown all sides. Remove to slow cooker. Drain excess fat from skillet.

2. Add onion to skillet; cook and stir about 5 minutes or until tender. Add caraway seeds, garlic powder and pepper; cook 15 minutes. Add onion mixture to slow cooker.

3. Add water to skillet, stirring to scrape up browned bits from bottom of skillet. Pour liquid into slow cooker. Partially drain sauerkraut, leaving some liquid; pour over meat in slow cooker. Top with potatoes.

4. Cover; cook on LOW 6 to 8 hours or until potatoes are tender, stirring once during cooking.

BAKED POTATO SOUP

Makes 6 to 8 servings

- 3 medium russet potatoes (about 1 pound)
- 1/4 cup (1/2 stick) butter
- 1 cup chopped onion
- 1/2 cup all-purpose flour
- 4 cups chicken or vegetable broth
- 1 1/2 cups instant mashed potato flakes
- 1 cup water
- 1 cup half-and-half
- 1 teaspoon salt
- 1/2 teaspoon dried basil
- 1/2 teaspoon dried thyme
- 1/4 teaspoon black pepper
- 1 cup (4 ounces) shredded Cheddar cheese
- 4 slices bacon, crisp-cooked and crumbled
- 1 green onion, chopped

1. Preheat oven to 400°F. Scrub potatoes and prick in several places with fork. Place in baking pan; bake 1 hour. Cool completely; peel and cut into 1/2-inch cubes. (Potatoes can be prepared several days in advance; refrigerate until ready to use.)

2. Melt butter in large saucepan or Dutch oven over medium heat. Add onion; cook and stir 3 minutes or until softened. Whisk in flour; cook and stir 1 minute. Gradually whisk in broth until well blended. Stir in mashed potato flakes, water, half-and-half, salt, basil, thyme and pepper; bring to a boil over medium-high heat. Reduce heat to medium; cook 5 minutes.

3. Stir in baked potato cubes; cook 10 to 15 minutes or until soup is thickened and heated through. Ladle into bowls; top with cheese, bacon and green onion.

GARDEN VEGETABLE SOUP

Makes 8 to 10 servings

1 tablespoon olive oil

1 medium onion, chopped

1 carrot, chopped

1 stalk celery, chopped

1 medium zucchini, diced

1 medium yellow squash, diced

1 red bell pepper, diced

2 tablespoons tomato paste

2 cloves garlic, minced

2 teaspoons salt

1 teaspoon Italian seasoning

$\frac{1}{2}$ teaspoon black pepper

8 cups vegetable broth

1 can (28 ounces) whole tomatoes, chopped, juice reserved

$\frac{1}{2}$ cup uncooked pearl barley

1 cup cut green beans (1-inch pieces)

$\frac{1}{2}$ cup corn

$\frac{1}{4}$ cup slivered fresh basil

1 tablespoon lemon juice

1. Heat oil in large saucepan or Dutch oven over medium-high heat. Add onion, carrot and celery; cook and stir 8 minutes or until vegetables are softened. Add zucchini, yellow squash and bell pepper; cook and stir 5 minutes or until softened. Stir in tomato paste, garlic, salt, Italian seasoning and black pepper; cook 1 minute. Stir in broth and tomatoes with juice; bring to a boil. Stir in barley.

2. Reduce heat to low; cook 30 minutes, stirring occasionally. Stir in green beans and corn; cook about 15 minutes or until barley is tender and green beans are crisp-tender. Stir in basil and lemon juice.

CHICKEN NOODLE SOUP

Makes 8 servings

- 2 **tablespoons butter**
- 1 **cup chopped onion**
- 1 **cup sliced carrots**
- ½ **cup diced celery**
- 2 **tablespoons vegetable oil**
- 1 **pound chicken breast tenderloins**
- 1 **pound chicken thigh fillets or boneless skinless chicken thighs**
- 4 **cups chicken broth, divided**
- 2 **cups water**
- 1 **tablespoon minced fresh parsley, plus additional for garnish**
- 1½ **teaspoons salt**
- ½ **teaspoon black pepper**
- 3 **cups uncooked egg noodles**

1. Melt butter in large saucepan or Dutch oven over medium-low heat. Add onion, carrots and celery; cook 15 minutes or until vegetables are soft, stirring occasionally.

2. Meanwhile, heat oil in large skillet over medium-high heat. Add chicken in single layer; cook 12 minutes or until lightly browned and cooked through, turning once. Remove chicken to cutting board. Add 1 cup broth to skillet; cook 1 minute, stirring to scrape up browned bits. Add broth to vegetables in saucepan. Stir in remaining 3 cups broth, water, 1 tablespoon parsley, salt and pepper.

3. Chop chicken into 1-inch pieces when cool enough to handle. Add to soup; bring to a boil over medium-high heat. Reduce heat to medium-low; cook 15 minutes. Add noodles; cook 15 minutes or until noodles are tender. Ladle into bowls; garnish with additional parsley.

Soups & Stews

BEEF VEGETABLE SOUP

Makes 6 to 8 servings

1½ pounds cubed beef stew
     meat

¼ cup all-purpose flour

3 tablespoons vegetable oil,
    divided

1 onion, chopped

2 stalks celery, chopped

3 tablespoons tomato paste

2 teaspoons salt

1 teaspoon dried thyme

½ teaspoon garlic powder

¼ teaspoon black pepper

6 cups beef broth, divided

1 can (28 ounces) stewed
    tomatoes

1 tablespoon Worcestershire
    sauce

1 bay leaf

4 red potatoes (about
    1 pound), cut into
    1-inch pieces

3 medium carrots, cut in half
    lengthwise and cut into
    ½-inch slices

6 ounces green beans,
    trimmed and cut into
    1-inch pieces

1 cup frozen corn

1. Combine beef and flour in medium bowl; toss to coat. Heat 1 tablespoon oil in large saucepan or Dutch oven over medium-high heat. Cook beef in two batches 5 minutes or until browned on all sides, adding additional 1 tablespoon oil after first batch. Transfer beef to medium bowl.

2. Heat remaining 1 tablespoon oil in same saucepan. Add onion and celery; cook and stir 5 minutes or until softened. Add tomato paste, salt, thyme, garlic powder and pepper; cook and stir 1 minute. Stir in 1 cup broth, stirring to scrape up browned bits from bottom of saucepan. Stir in remaining 5 cups broth, tomatoes with juice, Worcestershire sauce, bay leaf and beef; bring to a boil.

3. Reduce heat to low; cover and simmer 1 hour and 20 minutes. Add potatoes and carrots; cook 15 minutes. Add green beans and corn; cook 15 minutes or until vegetables are tender. Remove and discard bay leaf.

Soups & Stews

CHICKEN AND CORN CHOWDER

Makes 4 servings

1 tablespoon olive oil

1 pound boneless skinless chicken breasts, cut into 1/2-inch pieces

3 cups thawed frozen corn

1 medium onion, chopped

1 to 2 tablespoons water

1 cup diced carrots

2 tablespoons finely chopped jalapeño pepper (optional)

1/2 teaspoon dried oregano

1/4 teaspoon dried thyme

3 cups chicken broth

1 1/2 cups milk

1/2 teaspoon salt

1. Heat oil in large saucepan over medium heat. Add chicken; cook and stir about 10 minutes or until browned and no longer pink in center. Transfer chicken to bowl.

2. Add corn and onion to saucepan; cook and stir about 5 minutes or until onion is tender. Place 1 cup corn mixture and water in food processor or blender; process until puréed.

3. Add carrots, jalapeño pepper, if desired, oregano and thyme to saucepan; cook and stir about 5 minutes or until corn begins to brown. Return chicken to saucepan. Stir in broth, milk, puréed corn mixture and salt; bring to a boil. Reduce heat to low; cover and simmer 15 to 20 minutes to blend flavors.

BEEF STEW
Makes 8 servings

2 **tablespoons olive or vegetable oil**

3 **pounds boneless beef chuck, trimmed and cut into 2-inch chunks or cubed beef stew meat**

2 **teaspoons salt**

½ **teaspoon black pepper**

3 **sweet or yellow onions, halved and sliced**

6 **carrots, cut into ½-inch pieces**

8 **ounces sliced mushrooms**

¼ **pound smoked ham, cut into ¼-inch pieces**

2 **tablespoons minced garlic**

2 **cans (about 14 ounces each) beef broth**

1 **teaspoon sugar**

1 **teaspoon herbes de Provence or dried thyme**

1 **teaspoon Worcestershire sauce**

⅓ **cup cold water**

2 **tablespoons cornstarch**

3 **tablespoons chopped fresh parsley**

Hot cooked noodles or red potatoes (optional)

1. Heat oil in Dutch oven over medium-high heat. Add half of beef; sprinkle with 1 teaspoon salt and ¼ teaspoon pepper. Cook about 8 minutes or until browned on all sides. Transfer to bowl. Repeat with remaining beef, salt and pepper.

2. Add onions; cook and stir over medium heat 10 minutes. Stir in carrots, mushrooms, ham and garlic; cook and stir 10 minutes or until vegetables are softened, stirring to scrape up browned bits from bottom of Dutch oven.

3. Return beef to Dutch oven and pour in broth. (Liquid should just cover beef and vegetables; add water if needed.) Stir in sugar, herbes de Provence and Worcestershire sauce; bring to a boil. Reduce heat to low; cover and simmer 2 hours or until beef is fork-tender.

4. Skim fat from top of stew. Stir water into cornstarch in small bowl until smooth. Stir into stew; simmer 5 minutes. Stir in parsley. Serve over noodles, if desired.

Soups & Stews

CREAMY SHAKER CHICKEN SOUP

Makes 10 to 12 servings

13 **cups chicken broth, divided**

¼ **cup (½ stick) butter**

1 **cup whipping cream**

1 **package (12 ounces) uncooked egg noodles**

1 **cup thinly sliced celery**

1½ **cups water**

¾ **cup all-purpose flour**

2 **cups diced cooked chicken**

Salt and black pepper

¼ **cup finely chopped fresh parsley (optional)**

1. Combine 1 cup broth and butter in small saucepan. Bring to a boil over high heat. Continue to boil 15 to 20 minutes or until liquid is reduced to ¼ cup and has a syrupy consistency. Stir in cream. Set aside.

2. Bring remaining 12 cups broth to a boil in Dutch oven. Add noodles and celery; cook until noodles are just tender.

3. Whisk water and flour in medium bowl until smooth. Stir into broth mixture. Boil 2 minutes, stirring constantly.

4. Stir in reserved cream mixture; add chicken. Season to taste with salt and pepper. Heat just to serving temperature. *Do not boil.* Sprinkle with parsley, if desired.

Soups & Stews

SPLIT PEA SOUP

Makes 6 servings

- **1 package (16 ounces) dried green or yellow split peas**
- **7 cups water**
- **1 pound smoked ham hocks** *or* **4 ounces smoked sausage links, sliced and quartered**
- **2 carrots, chopped**
- **1 onion, chopped**
- **³/₄ teaspoon salt**
- **¹/₂ teaspoon dried basil**
- **¹/₄ teaspoon dried oregano**
- **¹/₄ teaspoon black pepper**

1. Rinse split peas thoroughly in colander under cold running water; discard any debris or blemished peas.

2. Combine peas, water, ham hocks, carrots, onion, salt, basil, oregano and pepper in large saucepan or Dutch oven; bring to a boil over high heat. Reduce heat to medium-low. Simmer 1 hour 15 minutes or until peas are tender, stirring occasionally. Stir frequently near end of cooking to prevent soup from scorching.

3. Remove ham hocks to large cutting board; let stand until cool enough to handle. Remove ham from hocks; chop meat and discard bones.

4. Place 3 cups soup in blender or food processor; blend until smooth. Return to saucepan; stir in ham. If soup is too thick, add water until desired consistency is reached. Cook just until heated through.

Soups & Stews

SALADS & SIDES

SPINACH SALAD WITH HOT APPLE DRESSING

Makes 6 servings

6 slices bacon

¾ cup apple cider

2 tablespoons packed brown sugar

1 tablespoon plus 1 teaspoon cider vinegar

¼ teaspoon black pepper

6 cups packed fresh spinach

2 cups sliced fresh mushrooms

1 medium tomato, cut into wedges

½ cup thinly sliced red onion

1. Cook bacon in medium skillet over medium heat about 10 minutes or until crisp, turning occasionally. Remove to paper towels to drain. Discard drippings.

2. Coarsely chop three bacon slices; set aside. Finely chop remaining three slices; return to skillet. Add apple cider, brown sugar, vinegar and pepper. Bring to a simmer over medium heat; remove from heat.

3. Combine spinach, mushrooms, tomato and onion in large bowl. Add dressing; toss to coat. Top with reserved bacon.

MASHED ROOT VEGETABLES

Makes 6 servings

1 **pound russet potatoes, peeled and cut into 1-inch pieces**

1 **pound turnips, peeled and cut into 1-inch pieces**

12 **ounces sweet potatoes, peeled and cut into 1-inch pieces**

8 **ounces parsnips, peeled and cut into ½-inch pieces**

1 **cup water**

5 **tablespoons butter**

2 **teaspoons salt**

¼ **teaspoon black pepper**

1 **cup milk**

1. Combine russet potatoes, turnips, sweet potatoes, parsnips, water, butter, salt and pepper in Dutch oven or large saucepan. Cover and bring to a boil over medium-high heat. Reduce heat; simmer 30 to 40 minutes or until vegetables are very tender, adding additional water if saucepan is dry.

2. Mash mixture with potato masher until smooth. Stir in milk. Cook over low heat 5 minutes, stirring frequently.

CORN PUDDING

Makes 8 servings

1 tablespoon butter

1 small onion, chopped

1 tablespoon all-purpose flour

2 cups half-and-half

1 cup milk

¼ cup quick-cooking grits or polenta

2 cups corn

4 eggs, lightly beaten

1 can (4 ounces) diced mild green chiles, drained

¾ teaspoon salt

¼ teaspoon black pepper

¼ teaspoon hot pepper sauce

1. Preheat oven to 325°F. Grease 11×7-inch baking dish.

2. Melt butter in large saucepan over medium heat. Add onion; cook and stir 5 minutes or until tender and lightly browned.

3. Stir in flour; cook until lightly browned. Stir in half-and-half and milk; bring to a boil. Whisk in grits; reduce heat to medium-low. Cook and stir 10 minutes or until mixture is thickened. Remove from heat. Stir in corn, eggs, chiles, salt, black pepper and hot pepper sauce. Pour into prepared baking dish.

4. Bake 1 hour or until knife inserted into center comes out clean.

GREENS AND PEARS WITH MAPLE-MUSTARD DRESSING

Makes 4 servings

- ¼ **cup maple syrup**
- 1 **tablespoon Dijon mustard**
- 1 **tablespoon olive oil**
- 1 **tablespoon balsamic or cider vinegar**
- ¼ **teaspoon salt**
- ⅛ **teaspoon black pepper**
- 4 **cups torn mixed salad greens**
- 1 **medium red pear, cored and thinly sliced**
- ¼ **cup sliced green onions**
- 3 **tablespoons dried cherries**
- 3 **tablespoons chopped walnuts, toasted***

*To toast walnuts, cook in medium skillet over medium heat 3 to 4 minutes or until lightly browned and fragrant, stirring frequently.

1. Whisk maple syrup, mustard, oil, vinegar, salt and pepper in small bowl until well blended.
2. Combine greens, pear, green onions, cherries and walnuts in large serving bowl. Drizzle with dressing; gently toss to coat.

Salads & Sides

CABBAGE AND RED POTATO SALAD

Makes 4 servings

- **1 pound baby red potatoes, quartered**
- **½ cup finely chopped cilantro**
- **2 tablespoons fresh lime juice**
- **2 tablespoons olive oil**
- **2 teaspoons honey**
- **½ teaspoon salt**
- **½ teaspoon ground cumin**
- **2 cups sliced napa cabbage**
- **2 cups sliced red cabbage**
- **½ cup sliced green onions**
- **2 tablespoons sunflower kernels**

1. Bring medium saucepan of salted water to a boil. Add potatoes; cook 10 minutes or until fork-tender. Drain and run under cold water to stop cooking.

2. Meanwhile, whisk cilantro, lime juice, oil, honey, salt and cumin in large bowl until smooth and well blended. Let stand 30 minutes to allow flavors to blend.

3. Add napa cabbage, red cabbage, potatoes and green onions to dressing; toss to coat evenly. Sprinkle with sunflower kernels just before serving.

ZUCCHINI CHOW CHOW

Makes about 6 cups

 2 **cups thinly sliced zucchini**

 2 **cups thinly sliced yellow summer squash***

 ½ **cup thinly sliced red onion**
  Salt

 1½ **cups cider vinegar**

 1 **to 1¼ cups sugar**

 1½ **tablespoons pickling spice**

 1 **cup thinly sliced carrots**

 1 **small red bell pepper, thinly sliced**

 *If yellow summer squash is not available, increase zucchini to 4 cups.

1. Place zucchini, summer squash and onion in colander. Sprinkle lightly with salt; let stand 30 minutes. Rinse well with cold water; drain thoroughly. Pat dry with paper towels.

2. Combine vinegar, sugar and pickling spice in medium saucepan. Bring to a boil over high heat. Add carrots and bell pepper; return to a boil. Remove from heat; cool to room temperature.

3. Spoon zucchini and summer squash into jars with tight-fitting lids. Using slotted spoon, transfer carrots and bell pepper to jars. Pour pickling liquid over vegetables in jars. Cover and refrigerate up to 3 weeks.

Salads & Sides

CLASSIC MACARONI SALAD

Makes 6 to 8 servings

- **2 cups uncooked elbow macaroni**
- **1 cup mayonnaise**
- **½ cup plain yogurt or sour cream**
- **3 tablespoons sweet pickle relish**
- **1 tablespoon yellow mustard**
- **2 teaspoons dried dill weed**
- **1 teaspoon salt**
- **1½ cups thawed frozen peas**
- **1 cup chopped green bell pepper**
- **1 cup thinly sliced celery**
- **8 ounces ham, cubed**
- **1 cup (4 ounces) shredded Cheddar cheese, divided**

1. Cook pasta in large saucepan of salted boiling water according to package directions for al dente. Drain and rinse under cold water until cool. Transfer to large serving bowl.

2. Meanwhile, combine mayonnaise, yogurt, relish, mustard, dill and salt in medium bowl; stir until well blended.

3. Add peas, bell pepper, celery and ham to pasta; mix well. Add mayonnaise mixture; mix well. Stir in ½ cup cheese; sprinkle with remaining ½ cup cheese. Serve immediately or cover and refrigerate until ready to serve.

CHICKEN, PEACH AND CABBAGE SALAD

Makes 6 servings

- **3 cups diced cooked chicken**
- **2 cups shredded red cabbage**
- **2 medium ripe peaches, peeled, pitted and cut into 1-inch pieces**
- **2 stalks celery, diced**
- **½ cup plain yogurt or sour cream**
- **6 tablespoons peach nectar or orange juice**
- **½ teaspoon salt**
- **½ teaspoon curry powder**
- **¼ teaspoon black pepper**

1. Combine chicken, cabbage, peaches and celery in medium bowl.
2. Stir together yogurt, peach nectar, salt, curry powder and pepper in small bowl. Stir into salad; mix well. Refrigerate until ready to serve.

APRICOT-GLAZED BEETS
Makes 4 servings

1 **pound fresh beets**

1 **cup apricot nectar**

1 **tablespoon cornstarch**

2 **tablespoons cider vinegar or red wine vinegar**

8 **dried apricot halves, cut into strips**

¼ **teaspoon salt**

1. Cut tops off beets, leaving at least 1 inch of stems (do not trim root ends). Scrub beets under running water with soft vegetable brush, being careful not to break skins. Place beets in medium saucepan; cover with water. Bring to a boil over high heat; reduce heat. Cover and simmer about 20 minutes or until just barely firm when pierced with fork. Transfer to plate to cool.

2. Combine apricot nectar and cornstarch in same saucepan. Add vinegar; stir until smooth. Add apricot strips and salt. Cook over medium heat until mixture thickens.

3. Cut roots and stems from beets on plate.* Peel, halve and cut beets into ¼-inch-thick slices. Add beet slices to apricot mixture; toss gently to coat.

Do not cut beets on cutting board; the juice will stain the board.

HEARTY HASH BROWN CASSEROLE
Makes about 16 servings

2 cups sour cream

2 cups (8 ounces) shredded Colby cheese, divided

1 can (10¾ ounces) cream of chicken or celery soup

½ cup (1 stick) butter, melted

1 small onion, finely chopped

¾ teaspoon salt

½ teaspoon black pepper

1 package (30 ounces) frozen shredded hash brown potatoes, thawed

1. Preheat oven to 375°F. Grease 13×9-inch baking dish.

2. Combine sour cream, 1½ cups cheese, soup, butter, onion, salt and pepper in large bowl; mix well. Add potatoes; stir until well blended. Spread mixture in prepared baking dish. (Do not pack down.) Sprinkle with remaining ½ cup cheese.

3. Bake 45 minutes or until cheese is melted and top of casserole is beginning to brown.

Salads & Sides

PUMPKIN MAC AND CHEESE
Makes 6 to 8 servings

1 package (16 ounces) uncooked large elbow macaroni or medium shell pasta

$\frac{1}{2}$ cup (1 stick) butter, divided

$\frac{1}{4}$ cup all-purpose flour

$1\frac{1}{2}$ cups milk

1 teaspoon salt, divided

$\frac{1}{4}$ teaspoon ground nutmeg

$\frac{1}{8}$ teaspoon ground red pepper

2 cups (8 ounces) shredded Cheddar cheese

2 cups (8 ounces) shredded Monterey Jack cheese, divided

1 cup canned pumpkin

1 cup panko bread crumbs

$\frac{1}{2}$ cup chopped hazelnuts or walnuts (optional)

$\frac{1}{8}$ teaspoon dried sage

1. Preheat oven to 350°F. Grease 2-quart baking dish. Cook macaroni in large saucepan of salted boiling water according to package directions for al dente. Drain and return to saucepan; keep warm.

2. Melt $\frac{1}{4}$ cup butter in medium saucepan over medium-high heat. Whisk in flour until smooth. Cook 1 minute without browning, whisking constantly. Gradually whisk in milk in thin steady stream. Add $\frac{3}{4}$ teaspoon salt, nutmeg and red pepper; cook 2 to 3 minutes or until thickened, stirring frequently. Gradually add Cheddar and 1 cup Monterey Jack cheeses, stirring after each addition until smooth. Add pumpkin; cook 1 minute or until heated through, stirring constantly. Pour sauce over pasta; stir to coat.

3. Melt remaining $\frac{1}{4}$ cup butter in small skillet over medium-low heat; cook until golden brown. Remove from heat; stir in panko, hazelnuts, if desired, sage and remaining $\frac{1}{4}$ teaspoon salt.

4. Spread half of pasta in prepared baking dish; sprinkle with $\frac{1}{2}$ cup Monterey Jack cheese. Top with remaining pasta; sprinkle with remaining $\frac{1}{2}$ cup Monterey Jack cheese. Top with panko mixture.

5. Bake 25 to 30 minutes or until topping is golden brown and pasta is heated through.

Salads & Sides

BANANA MONKEY BREAD
Makes 12 servings

2 ripe bananas

2 cups all-purpose flour, divided

¾ cup whole wheat flour

½ cup old-fashioned oats

¾ cup sugar, divided

¼ cup warm milk (120°F)

3 tablespoons vegetable or canola oil

1 package (¼ ounce) instant or rapid-rise active dry yeast

1 teaspoon salt

2 teaspoons ground cinnamon, divided

5 tablespoons butter, melted, divided

1. Place bananas in large bowl of stand mixer. Beat with paddle attachment at low speed 1 minute or until bananas are mashed. Add ¼ cup all-purpose flour, whole wheat flour, oats, ¼ cup sugar, milk, oil, yeast, salt and 1 teaspoon cinnamon. Beat at medium speed 3 minutes.

2. Replace paddle attachment with dough hook; beat in enough remaining all-purpose flour to form soft dough. Knead at low speed 5 minutes or until dough is smooth and elastic. Shape dough into a ball. Place in greased bowl; turn to grease top. Cover; let rise in warm place about 1 hour or until doubled in size.

3. Brush 12-cup (10-inch) bundt pan with 1 tablespoon butter. Place remaining 4 tablespoons butter in small bowl. Combine remaining ½ cup sugar and 1 teaspoon cinnamon in medium bowl. Turn out dough onto lightly floured surface; pat into 9-inch square. Cut into 1-inch squares; roll into balls. Dip balls in butter; roll in cinnamon-sugar to coat. Layer in prepared pan. Cover; let rise 1 hour or until dough is puffy. Preheat oven to 350°F.

4. Bake 30 minutes or until bread is firm and golden brown. Loosen edges of bread with knife; immediately invert onto serving plate. Cool slightly before serving.

CRANBERRY PUMPKIN NUT BREAD

Makes 1 loaf

2 cups all-purpose flour

2 teaspoons pumpkin pie spice

1 teaspoon baking powder

½ teaspoon baking soda

½ teaspoon salt

1 cup canned pumpkin

¾ cup granulated sugar

½ cup packed brown sugar

2 eggs

⅓ cup vegetable or canola oil

1 cup chopped dried cranberries

¾ cup chopped macadamia nuts, toasted*

*To toast macadamia nuts, spread in single layer on baking sheet. Bake in preheated 350°F oven 8 to 10 minutes or until lightly browned and fragrant, stirring occasionally.

1. Preheat oven to 350°F. Grease 9×5-inch loaf pan.

2. Whisk flour, pumpkin pie spice, baking powder, baking soda and salt in large bowl. Combine pumpkin, granulated sugar, brown sugar, eggs and oil in medium bowl; stir until well blended. Add to flour mixture; stir just until dry ingredients are moistened. Stir in cranberries and nuts. Pour batter into prepared pan.

3. Bake 45 to 50 minutes or until toothpick inserted into center comes out clean. Cool in pan 15 minutes. Remove to wire rack; cool completely.

Breads & Muffins

SUGAR AND SPICE BREAD

Makes 1 loaf

  1 cup milk

  ¼ cup (½ stick) butter

  3 cups bread flour, divided

  ¼ cup packed brown sugar

  1 package (¼ ounce) instant or rapid-rise active dry yeast

  2 teaspoons ground cinnamon

  1 teaspoon salt

  ¼ teaspoon ground nutmeg

  ⅛ teaspoon ground cloves

1. Combine milk and butter in small saucepan; heat to 120°F. Whisk 1 cup flour, brown sugar, yeast, cinnamon, salt, nutmeg and cloves in large bowl of electric stand mixer. Add milk mixture to flour mixture; beat at medium speed 2 minutes with paddle attachment.

2. Replace paddle attachment with dough hook; beat in enough remaining flour until soft dough forms. Knead at medium-low speed 5 to 8 minutes or until dough is smooth and elastic. Place dough in large lightly greased bowl; turn to grease top. Cover and let rise in warm place about 45 minutes or until doubled in size.

3. Grease 9×5-inch loaf pan. Punch down dough. Shape dough into loaf; place in prepared pan. Cover and let rise in warm place about 30 minutes or until doubled in size. Preheat oven to 375°F.

4. Bake 35 to 40 minutes or until browned and loaf sounds hollow when tapped (internal temperature of 200°F). Remove to wire rack; cool completely before slicing.

ENGLISH-STYLE SCONES

Makes 6 scones

3 eggs, divided

¹/₂ cup whipping cream

1¹/₂ teaspoons vanilla

2 cups all-purpose flour

2 teaspoons baking powder

¹/₄ teaspoon salt

¹/₄ cup (¹/₂ stick) cold butter, cut into ¹/₄-inch pieces

¹/₄ cup finely chopped pitted dates

¹/₄ cup golden raisins or currants

1 teaspoon water

6 tablespoons orange marmalade fruit spread

6 tablespoons softly whipped cream or crème fraîche

1. Preheat oven to 375°F. Line large baking sheet with parchment paper.

2. Whisk 2 eggs, cream and vanilla in medium bowl until blended. Combine flour, baking powder and salt in medium bowl. Cut in butter with pastry blender or fingertips until mixture resembles coarse crumbs. Stir in dates and raisins. Add cream mixture; stir just until dry ingredients are moistened.

3. Turn out dough onto lightly floured surface; knead four times with floured hands. Place dough on prepared baking sheet; pat into 8-inch circle. Gently score dough into six wedges with sharp wet knife, cutting three-fourths of the way through dough. Beat remaining egg and water in small bowl; brush lightly over dough.

4. Bake 18 to 20 minutes or until golden brown. Remove to wire rack; cool 5 minutes. Cut into wedges. Serve warm with marmalade and whipped cream.

SIMPLE GOLDEN CORN BREAD
Makes 9 to 12 servings

1¼ cups all-purpose flour

¾ cup yellow cornmeal

⅓ cup sugar

2 teaspoons baking powder

1 teaspoon salt

1¼ cups whole milk

¼ cup (½ stick) butter, melted

1 egg

Honey Butter (recipe follows, optional)

1. Preheat oven to 400°F. Grease 8-inch square baking dish.

2. Combine flour, cornmeal, sugar, baking powder and salt in large bowl; mix well. Beat milk, butter and egg in medium bowl until well blended. Add to flour mixture; stir just until dry ingredients are moistened. Pour batter into prepared baking dish.

3. Bake 25 minutes or until golden brown and toothpick inserted into center comes out clean. Prepare Honey Butter, if desired. Serve with corn bread.

HONEY BUTTER: Beat 6 tablespoons (¾ stick) softened butter and ¼ cup honey in medium bowl with electric mixer at medium-high speed until light and creamy.

Breads & Muffins

BUTTERMILK BISCUITS

Makes about 9 biscuits

2 cups all-purpose flour

1 tablespoon baking powder

2 teaspoons sugar

$1/2$ teaspoon salt

$1/2$ teaspoon baking soda

$1/2$ cup (1 stick) cold butter, cut into $1/4$-inch pieces

$2/3$ cup buttermilk*

*Or substitute soured fresh milk. To sour milk, combine 2$1/2$ teaspoons lemon juice plus enough milk to equal $2/3$ cup. Stir; let stand 5 minutes before using.

1. Preheat oven to 450°F.

2. Combine flour, baking powder, sugar, salt and baking soda in medium bowl. Cut in butter with pastry blender or fingertips until mixture resembles coarse crumbs. Make well in center of dry ingredients. Add buttermilk; stir until mixture forms soft dough that clings together and forms a ball.

3. Turn out dough onto well-floured surface; knead gently 10 to 12 times. Roll or pat dough to $1/2$-inch thickness. Cut out biscuits with floured 2$1/2$-inch round cutter. Place 2 inches apart on ungreased baking sheet.

4. Bake 8 to 10 minutes or until golden brown. Serve warm.

DROP BISCUITS: Prepare biscuits as directed in step 2, increasing buttermilk to 1 cup. Stir batter with wooden spoon about 15 strokes. *Do not knead.* Drop dough by heaping tablespoonfuls 1 inch apart onto greased baking sheets. Bake as directed in step 4. Makes about 18 biscuits.

SOUR CREAM DILL BISCUITS: Prepare biscuits as directed in step 2, omitting buttermilk. Combine $1/2$ cup sour cream, $1/3$ cup milk and 1 tablespoon chopped fresh dill *or* 1 teaspoon dried dill weed in small bowl until well blended. Add to flour mixture; continue as directed.

Breads & Muffins

ORANGE CRANBERRY MUFFINS
Makes 8 muffins

½ cup dried cranberries

3 tablespoons packed brown sugar

1 cup orange juice

1 egg

2 tablespoons canola or vegetable oil

1 cup whole wheat flour

½ cup all-purpose flour

1½ teaspoons baking powder

½ teaspoon ground cinnamon

¼ teaspoon salt

¼ teaspoon ground nutmeg

1. Preheat oven to 400°F. Grease 8 standard (2½-inch) muffin cups or line with paper baking cups. Combine cranberries and brown sugar in small bowl. Stir in orange juice, egg, salt and oil; let stand 5 minutes.

2. Combine whole wheat flour, all-purpose flour, baking powder, cinnamon, salt and nutmeg in medium bowl. Add cranberry mixture to flour mixture; stir just until combined. Spoon batter into prepared muffin cups, filling three-fourths full.

3. Bake 18 to 20 minutes or until toothpick inserted into centers comes out clean. Immediately remove from pan to wire rack. Serve warm or cool completely.

OATMEAL RAISIN NUT BREAD
Makes 1 loaf

- **2 to 2½ cups bread flour, divided**
- **1 cup old-fashioned oats**
- **1 package (¼ ounce) instant or rapid-rise active dry yeast**
- **1½ teaspoons salt**
- **1½ teaspoons ground cinnamon**
- **1 cup plus 2 tablespoons warm water (120°F)**
- **¼ cup maple syrup**
- **2 tablespoons vegetable oil**
- **1 cup raisins**
- **¾ cup chopped pecans**

1. Combine 1 cup flour, oats, yeast, salt and cinnamon in large bowl of stand mixer. Combine warm water, maple syrup and oil in medium bowl. Add to flour mixture; beat with paddle attachment at medium speed 3 minutes.

2. Replace paddle attachment with dough hook. Add enough remaining flour, ½ cup at a time, to form soft dough. Knead at low speed 6 minutes or until dough is smooth and elastic. Add raisins and pecans; mix until incorporated. Shape dough into a ball. Place dough in large lightly greased bowl; turn to grease top. Cover and let rise in warm place about 45 minutes or until doubled in size.

3. Grease 9×5-inch loaf pan. Punch down dough. Roll out dough into 14×8-inch rectangle on lightly floured surface. Starting with short side, tightly roll up dough; pinch seam to seal. Place seam side down in prepared pan. Cover and let rise about 30 minutes or until doubled in size. Preheat oven to 375°F.

4. Bake 30 to 40 minutes or until top is browned and loaf sounds hollow when tapped (internal temperature of 190°F). Remove from pan to wire rack; cool completely before slicing.

Breads & Muffins

HERBED POTATO ROLLS
Makes 12 rolls

2³/₄ cups bread flour, divided

¹/₂ cup instant mashed
potato flakes

1 tablespoon sugar

1 package (¹/₄ ounce) instant
or rapid-rise active dry
yeast

1¹/₄ teaspoons dried rosemary

1 teaspoon salt

¹/₄ teaspoon black pepper

1 cup warm milk (120°F)

1¹/₂ tablespoons olive oil

1 egg, beaten

Poppy seeds, sesame seeds
and/or additional dried
rosemary (optional)

1. Combine 1 cup flour, potato flakes, sugar, yeast, rosemary, salt and pepper in large bowl of electric stand mixer. Add milk and oil; beat with paddle attachment at medium speed 2 minutes.

2. Replace paddle attachment with dough hook. With mixer running at low speed, add enough remaining flour to form soft dough. Knead at medium-low speed 6 to 8 minutes or until dough is smooth and elastic. Place dough in large lightly greased bowl; turn to grease top. Cover and let rise in warm place about 45 minutes or until doubled in size.

3. Line large baking sheet with parchment paper. Punch down dough. Divide dough into 12 pieces; roll each piece into 10-inch rope on lightly floured surface. Shape rope into a coil, tucking end under coil. Place 2 inches apart on prepared baking sheet. Cover and let rise in warm place about 40 minutes or until doubled in size. Preheat oven to 375°F. Brush rolls with beaten egg; sprinkle with toppings, if desired.

4. Bake about 18 minutes or until golden brown. Remove to wire rack to cool. Serve warm or at room temperature.

RHUBARB BREAD
Makes 1 loaf

2 cups all-purpose flour

1 cup sugar

1 tablespoon baking powder

1 teaspoon salt

1/4 teaspoon ground cinnamon

1 cup milk

2 eggs

1/3 cup butter, melted

2 teaspoons grated fresh ginger (about 1 inch)

10 ounces chopped fresh rhubarb (1/4-inch pieces, about 2 1/4 cups total)

3/4 cup chopped walnuts, toasted*

*To toast walnuts, spread in single layer on baking sheet. Bake in preheated 350°F oven 5 to 7 minutes or until lightly browned and fragrant, stirring frequently.

1. Preheat oven to 350°F. Grease 9×5-inch loaf pan.

2. Combine flour, sugar, baking powder, salt and cinnamon in large bowl; mix well. Whisk milk, eggs, butter and ginger in medium bowl until well blended. Add to flour mixture; stir just until dry ingredients are moistened. Add rhubarb and walnuts; stir just until blended. Pour batter into prepared pan.

3. Bake 60 to 65 minutes or until toothpick inserted into center comes out clean. Cool in pan on wire rack 15 minutes. Remove from pan to wire rack; cool completely before slicing.

Breads & Muffins

HONEY BUTTER PULL-APART BREAD

Makes 8 servings

3 **cups all-purpose flour**

1 **package (¹/₄ ounce) instant or rapid-rise active dry yeast**

1 **teaspoon salt**

1 **cup warm water (120°F)**

2 **tablespoons butter, melted**

¹/₄ **cup (¹/₂ stick) butter, softened**

¹/₄ **cup honey**

1. Combine flour, yeast and salt in large bowl of stand mixer. Stir in warm water and melted butter with wooden spoon to form soft dough. Knead with dough hook at low speed 5 to 7 minutes or until dough is smooth and elastic.

2. Shape dough into a ball. Place in large lightly greased bowl; turn to grease top. Cover and let rise in warm place about 45 minutes or until doubled in size.

3. Grease 8×4-inch loaf pan. Combine softened butter and honey in small bowl; mix well.

4. Turn out dough onto lightly floured surface. Roll out dough into 18×10-inch rectangle; cut in half crosswise to make two 9×10-inch rectangles. Spread some of honey butter over one half of dough; top with remaining half. Cut dough in half crosswise to make two 9×5-inch rectangles. Spread some of honey butter over one half; top with remaining half. Cut dough in half lengthwise, then cut crosswise into 1-inch strips. Place rows of strips vertically in prepared pan.

5. Cover and let rise in warm place 1 hour or until dough is puffy. Preheat oven to 350°F. Brush or dollop remaining honey butter over dough strips.

6. Bake 30 minutes or until bread is firm and golden brown. Remove to wire rack to cool slightly. Serve warm.

Breads & Muffins

CINNAMON SPICED MUFFINS

Makes 36 mini muffins

1½ **cups all-purpose flour**

¾ **cup sugar, divided**

2 **teaspoons baking powder**

½ **teaspoon salt**

½ **teaspoon ground nutmeg**

½ **teaspoon ground coriander**

½ **teaspoon ground allspice**

½ **cup milk**

⅓ **cup butter, melted**

1 **egg**

1 **teaspoon ground cinnamon**

¼ **cup (½ stick) butter, melted**

1. Preheat oven to 400°F. Grease 36 mini (1¾-inch) muffin cups.

2. Combine flour, ½ cup sugar, baking powder, salt, nutmeg, coriander and allspice in large bowl. Combine milk, ⅓ cup melted butter and egg in small bowl; stir into flour mixture just until dry ingredients are moistened. Spoon evenly into prepared muffin cups.

3. Bake 10 minutes or until toothpick inserted into centers comes out clean. Cool in pan 10 minutes.

4. Meanwhile, combine remaining ¼ cup sugar and cinnamon in shallow dish. Dip warm muffin tops in ¼ cup melted butter, then in sugar-cinnamon mixture. Serve warm.

Breads & Muffins

COOKIES & BARS

COCOA BOTTOM BANANA PECAN BARS

Makes 2 to 3 dozen bars

1½ cups all-purpose flour

1 teaspoon baking powder

1 teaspoon baking soda

½ teaspoon salt

1 cup sugar

½ cup (1 stick) butter, softened

5 ripe bananas, mashed

1 egg

1 teaspoon vanilla

½ cup chopped pecans

¼ cup unsweetened cocoa powder

1. Preheat oven to 350°F. Grease 13×9-inch baking pan. Whisk flour, baking powder, baking soda and salt in medium bowl.

2. Beat sugar and butter in large bowl with electric mixer at medium speed until creamy. Add bananas, egg and vanilla; beat until well blended. Add flour mixture; beat at low speed until well blended. Stir in pecans.

3. Remove half of batter to medium bowl; stir in cocoa until blended. Spread chocolate batter in prepared pan. Top with plain batter; swirl with knife to marbleize.

4. Bake 30 to 35 minutes or until edges are lightly browned. Cool completely in pan on wire rack. Cut into bars.

HONEY SPICE BALLS

Makes about 2¹/₂ dozen cookies

½ cup (1 stick) butter, softened

½ cup packed brown sugar

1 egg

1 tablespoon honey

1 teaspoon vanilla

2 cups all-purpose flour

½ teaspoon baking powder

½ teaspoon ground cinnamon

¼ teaspoon ground nutmeg

½ cup quick oats

1. Preheat oven to 350°F. Grease cookie sheets or line with parchment paper.

2. Beat butter and brown sugar in large bowl with electric mixer at medium speed until creamy. Add egg, honey and vanilla; beat until light and fluffy. Stir in flour, baking powder, cinnamon and nutmeg until well blended.

3. Place oats in small bowl. Shape tablespoonfuls of dough into balls; roll in oats. Place 2 inches apart on prepared cookie sheets.

4. Bake 15 to 18 minutes or until cookie tops crack slightly. Cool on cookie sheets 1 minute. Remove to wire racks; cool completely.

Cookies & Bars

LEMON ICED AMBROSIA BARS

Makes 2 to 3 dozen bars

BARS

1³/₄ **cups all-purpose flour, divided**

¹/₃ **cup powdered sugar**

¹/₂ **teaspoon salt**

³/₄ **cup (1¹/₂ sticks) cold butter, cut into ¹/₄-inch pieces**

4 **eggs**

2 **cups packed brown sugar**

1 **cup flaked coconut**

1 **cup finely chopped pecans**

¹/₂ **teaspoon baking powder**

LEMON ICING

2 **cups powdered sugar**

3 **tablespoons lemon juice**

2 **tablespoons butter, softened**

1. Preheat oven to 350°F. Grease 13×9-inch baking pan.

2. Combine 1¹/₂ cups flour, ¹/₃ cup powdered sugar and salt in medium bowl; cut in butter with pastry blender or fingertips until mixture resembles coarse crumbs. Press onto bottom of prepared pan; bake 15 minutes.

3. Meanwhile, beat eggs in medium bowl. Add remaining ¹/₄ cup flour, brown sugar, coconut, pecans and baking powder in medium bowl; mix well. Spread evenly over baked crust; bake 20 minutes. Cool completely in pan on wire rack.

4. For icing, stir together 2 cups powdered sugar, lemon juice and 2 tablespoons butter until smooth. Spread over bars. Cover and refrigerate. Cut into bars. Store, covered, in refrigerator.

Cookies & Bars

PEANUT BUTTER FUDGE WHOOPIES

Makes 14 whoopie pies

1½ cups plus 2 tablespoons all-purpose flour

1 teaspoon baking powder

1 teaspoon baking soda

1 cup creamy peanut butter, divided

½ cup granulated sugar

½ cup packed brown sugar

¼ cup (½ stick) butter, softened

1 egg

1 teaspoon vanilla

½ cup milk

16 ounces semisweet chocolate, chopped

1½ cups whipping cream

½ cup chopped peanuts (optional)

1. For cookies, combine flour, baking powder and baking soda in medium bowl.

2. Beat ½ cup peanut butter, granulated sugar, brown sugar and butter in large bowl with electric mixer at medium-high speed until creamy. Add egg and vanilla; beat at medium speed 2 minutes. Add flour mixture and milk; beat at low speed just until combined. Cover and refrigerate 30 minutes.

3. Preheat oven to 350°F. Line two cookie sheets with parchment paper. Drop tablespoonfuls of batter 2 inches apart onto prepared cookie sheets.

4. Bake 14 minutes or until light brown around edges. Cool on cookie sheets 5 minutes. Remove to wire racks; cool completely.

5. For filling, place chocolate and remaining ½ cup peanut butter in large bowl. Bring cream to a simmer in small saucepan over low heat. Pour over chocolate and peanut butter. Let stand 2 minutes; stir until well blended. Refrigerate 30 minutes or until firm. Beat with electric mixer at medium-high speed until thick and creamy.

6. Pipe or spread filling on flat side of half of cookies; top with remaining cookies. Place peanuts in shallow dish; roll edges of cookies in peanuts, if desired.

FROSTED APPLE BUTTER COOKIES
Makes about 4¹/₂ dozen cookies

1 cup (2 sticks) butter, softened

¹/₂ **cup granulated sugar**

¹/₂ **cup packed brown sugar**

1 cup apple butter

1 teaspoon vanilla

1 egg

2 cups all-purpose flour

1 teaspoon baking powder

1 teaspoon baking soda

1 teaspoon ground cinnamon

¹/₄ **teaspoon salt**

³/₄ **cup chopped toasted* walnuts**

FROSTING

¹/₂ **cup packed brown sugar**

3 tablespoons butter

¹/₄ **cup whipping cream**

1¹/₂ **to 2 cups powdered sugar**

*To toast walnuts, spread in single layer on baking sheet. Bake in preheated 350°F oven 5 to 7 minutes or until lightly browned and fragrant, stirring occasionally.

1. Preheat oven to 350°F. Line cookie sheets with parchment paper.

2. Beat 1 cup butter, granulated sugar and ¹/₂ cup brown sugar in large bowl with electric mixer on medium speed until creamy. Add apple butter, egg and vanilla; beat again until light and fluffy. Gradually add flour, baking powder, baking soda, cinnamon and salt, beating at low speed until well blended; stir in nuts.

3. Drop dough by rounded teaspoonfuls 2 inches apart onto prepared cookie sheets. Bake 10 to 12 minutes or until lightly browned around edges. Remove to wire racks; cool completely.

4. For frosting, melt ¹/₂ cup brown sugar and 3 tablespoons butter in medium saucepan over medium-high heat, stirring frequently. Bring to a boil; cook 1 minute, stirring constantly or until slightly thickened. Remove from heat; cool 10 minutes.

5. Add cream; beat until smooth. Add 1¹/₂ cups powdered sugar, ¹/₄ cup at a time, beating well after each addition until frosting is desired consistency. Spread over cookies.

Cookies & Bars

SNICKERDOODLES

Makes about 3 dozen cookies

³/₄ cup plus 2 tablespoons sugar, divided

2 teaspoons ground cinnamon, divided

1¹/₃ cups all-purpose flour

1 teaspoon cream of tartar

¹/₂ teaspoon baking soda

¹/₂ teaspoon salt

¹/₂ cup (1 stick) butter, softened

1 egg

1. Preheat oven to 375°F. Line cookie sheets with parchment paper. Combine 2 tablespoons sugar and 1 teaspoon cinnamon in small bowl.

2. Combine flour, remaining 1 teaspoon cinnamon, cream of tartar, baking soda and salt in medium bowl.

3. Beat remaining ³/₄ cup sugar and butter in large bowl with electric mixer at medium speed until creamy. Beat in egg. Gradually add flour mixture, beating at low speed until stiff dough forms. Roll dough into 1-inch balls; roll in cinnamon-sugar mixture. Place on prepared cookie sheets.

4. Bake 10 minutes or until cookies are set. *Do not overbake.* Remove to wire racks; cool completely.

Cookies & Bars

DATE-FILLED COOKIES
Makes about 3 dozen cookies

2 cups chopped pitted dates

¾ cup water

1½ cups granulated sugar, divided

¼ cup chopped walnuts

3½ cups all-purpose flour

½ teaspoon salt

⅛ teaspoon ground cinnamon

1 cup (2 sticks) butter, softened

1 cup packed brown sugar

3 eggs

1 teaspoon vanilla

1. Preheat oven to 350°F. Grease cookie sheets or line with parchment paper.

2. Combine dates, water and ½ cup granulated sugar in medium saucepan; cook over medium heat until thick, stirring occasionally. Stir in walnuts; cool slightly.

3. Whisk flour, salt and cinnamon in medium bowl. Combine butter, remaining 1 cup granulated sugar and brown sugar in medium bowl. Beat with electric mixer at medium speed until creamy. Add eggs and vanilla; beat until light and fluffy. Gradually add flour mixture, beating just until blended.

4. Drop dough by rounded teaspoonfuls on prepared cookie sheets; top with about ½ teaspoon date mixture. Top with additional 1 teaspoon dough; flatten slightly to cover. Seal edges.

5. Bake 10 to 12 minutes or until lightly browned. Cool 1 minute on cookie sheets. Remove to wire racks; cool completely.

Cookies & Bars

CINNAMON RAISIN DELIGHTS

Makes about 1 dozen cookies

1¼ cups all-purpose flour

1 teaspoon ground cinnamon

½ teaspoon salt

½ teaspoon baking soda

½ cup (1 stick) butter, softened

½ cup packed brown sugar

¼ cup granulated sugar

1 egg, lightly beaten

1 teaspoon vanilla

1 cup raisins

¾ cup prepared vanilla frosting

1. Preheat oven to 350°F. Grease cookie sheets.

2. Combine flour, cinnamon, salt and baking soda in medium bowl. Beat butter, brown sugar and granulated sugar in large bowl with electric mixer at medium speed until light and fluffy. Add egg and vanilla; beat until well blended. Add flour mixture; beat just until blended. Stir in raisins.

3. Shape dough by rounded tablespoonfuls into balls; place 2 inches apart on prepared cookie sheets.

4. Bake 11 to 13 minutes or until edges are lightly browned. Cool on cookie sheets 2 minutes. Remove to wire racks; cool completely.

5. Spread 1 tablespoon frosting on flat side of one cookie; top with second cookie. Repeat with remaining cookies and frosting.

Cookies & Bars

MOLASSES SPICE COOKIES
Makes about 6 dozen cookies

2 cups all-purpose flour

2 teaspoons baking soda

1 teaspoon ground ginger

1 teaspoon ground cinnamon

1 teaspoon ground cloves

¼ teaspoon salt

¼ teaspoon dry mustard

1 cup granulated sugar

¾ cup (1½ sticks) butter, softened

¼ cup molasses

1 egg

½ cup granulated brown sugar* or granulated sugar

Granulated brown sugar is brown sugar that has been processed to have a light, dry texture similar to granulated sugar. It can be found in the baking aisles of most supermarkets.

1. Preheat oven to 375°F. Grease cookie sheets. Combine flour, baking soda, ginger, cinnamon, cloves, salt and mustard in medium bowl.

2. Beat granulated sugar and butter in large bowl with electric mixer at medium speed 5 minutes or until light and fluffy. Add molasses and egg; beat until blended. Add flour mixture; beat just until blended.

3. Place granulated brown sugar in shallow dish. Shape dough into 1-inch balls; roll in sugar to coat. Place 2 inches apart on prepared cookie sheets.

4. Bake 15 minutes or until lightly browned. Cool on cookie sheets 2 minutes. Remove to wire racks; cool completely.

APRICOT OATMEAL BARS
Makes 9 to 12 bars

1½ **cups old-fashioned oats**

1¼ **cups all-purpose flour**

½ **cup packed brown sugar**

1 **teaspoon ground ginger, divided**

½ **teaspoon salt**

½ **teaspoon baking soda**

½ **teaspoon ground cinnamon**

¾ **cup (1½ sticks) butter, melted**

1¼ **cups apricot preserves**

1. Preheat oven to 350°F. Line 8-inch square baking pan with foil or parchment paper, leaving 1-inch overhang on two sides.

2. Combine oats, flour, brown sugar, ½ teaspoon ginger, salt, baking soda and cinnamon in large bowl. Add butter; stir just until moistened and crumbly. Reserve 1½ cups oat mixture for topping. Press remaining oat mixture evenly onto bottom of prepared pan.

3. Combine preserves and remaining ½ teaspoon ginger in small bowl. Spread preserves evenly over crust; sprinkle with reserved oat mixture.

4. Bake 30 minutes or until golden brown. Cool completely in pan on wire rack. Remove from pan using foil. Cut into bars.

Cookies & Bars

APPLESAUCE FUDGE BARS
Makes 2 to 3 dozen bars

½ **cup (1 stick) butter**

3 **ounces semisweet chocolate, chopped**

1 **cup packed brown sugar**

²/₃ **cup unsweetened applesauce**

2 **eggs, beaten**

1 **teaspoon vanilla**

1 **cup all-purpose flour**

¼ **teaspoon baking powder**

¼ **teaspoon baking soda**

½ **cup walnuts, chopped**

1 **cup milk chocolate chips**

1. Preheat oven to 350°F. Grease 9-inch square baking pan.

2. Melt semisweet chocolate and butter in small heavy saucepan over low heat. Remove from heat; let stand 10 minutes.

3. Combine brown sugar, applesauce, eggs and vanilla in large bowl. Combine flour, baking powder and baking soda in small bowl; add to applesauce mixture. Stir in chocolate mixture. Spread batter evenly in prepared pan. Sprinkle with nuts.

4. Bake 25 to 30 minutes or just until set. Sprinkle chocolate chips over top. Let stand 2 minutes or until chips are melted; spread evenly over bars. Cool in pan on wire rack. Cut into bars.

Cookies & Bars

CAKES & PUDDINGS

APPLE BUTTER CAKE
Makes 12 servings

1 cup (2 sticks) plus
   2 tablespoons butter,
   softened, divided

3 cups all-purpose flour

1½ teaspoons baking powder

1 teaspoon salt

½ teaspoon baking soda

1½ teaspoons ground
   cinnamon

¾ teaspoon ground nutmeg

½ teaspoon ground allspice
   or cloves

2¾ cups granulated sugar

4 eggs

1 cup apple butter

1 tablespoon vanilla

1 cup sour cream

½ cup apple cider

Powdered sugar (optional)

1. Preheat oven to 350°F. Generously grease 10-inch tube pan with 2 tablespoons butter. Whisk flour, baking powder, salt, baking soda, cinnamon, nutmeg and allspice in medium bowl.

2. Beat remaining 1 cup butter and granulated sugar in large bowl with electric mixer at medium speed about 3 minutes or until light and fluffy. Add eggs, one at a time, beating well after each addition. Add apple butter and vanilla; beat until well blended. With mixer running on low speed, alternately add flour mixture, sour cream and cider; beat just until blended. Scrape bottom and side of bowl with spatula to bring batter together. Spoon batter into prepared pan; smooth top.

3. Bake 1 hour and 10 minutes or until wooden skewer inserted near center comes out with moist crumbs. Cool in pan on wire rack 20 minutes. Place serving plate on top of pan; carefully invert cake onto plate.

4. Just before serving, if desired, place 9-inch doily over cake. Sift powdered sugar over doily; carefully remove doily.

PUMPKIN CAKE WITH ORANGE GLAZE

Makes 16 to 24 servings

CAKE

- **2 cups all-purpose flour**
- **2 teaspoons baking powder**
- **2 teaspoons ground cinnamon**
- **1 teaspoon baking soda**
- **1 teaspoon salt**
- **1 teaspoon ground ginger**
- **1 teaspoon ground nutmeg**
- **1 can (15 ounces) pumpkin purée**
- **3 eggs**
- **¾ cup packed brown sugar**
- **½ cup granulated sugar**
- **½ cup unsweetened applesauce**
- **2 tablespoons vegetable oil**

GLAZE

- **2 ounces cream cheese, softened**
- **¼ cup powdered sugar**
- **2 to 4 tablespoons milk**
- **¼ teaspoon orange extract**

1. Preheat oven to 350°F. Grease 13×9-inch baking pan.

2. Combine flour, baking powder, cinnamon, baking soda, salt, ginger and nutmeg in medium bowl; mix well. Stir pumpkin, eggs, brown sugar, granulated sugar, applesauce and oil in large bowl until well blended. Gradually stir in flour mixture until smooth and well blended. Pour batter into prepared pan.

3. Bake 30 to 35 minutes or until toothpick inserted into center comes out clean. Cool completely in pan on wire rack.

4. For glaze, beat cream cheese in medium bowl until smooth. Add powdered sugar; beat until well blended. Add 2 tablespoons milk and orange extract; beat until smooth. Add additional milk, 1 teaspoon at a time, until desired consistency is reached.

5. Spread glaze over cake; let stand until set.

Cakes & Puddings

CHOCOLATE PUDDING PARFAITS

Makes 4 servings

- **2 ounces semisweet chocolate, chopped**
- **2 ounces white chocolate, chopped**
- **¹⁄₂ cup sugar**
- **2 tablespoons all-purpose flour**
- **1 tablespoon cornstarch**
- **2¹⁄₄ cups milk**
- **2 egg yolks, beaten**
- **2 teaspoons vanilla**

1. Place semisweet chocolate and white chocolate in separate heatproof bowls.

2. Whisk sugar, flour and cornstarch in small saucepan. Gradually whisk in milk. Cook over medium heat until mixture comes to a boil, whisking constantly. Boil 2 minutes, whisking constantly.

3. Remove saucepan from heat. Whisk small amount of hot milk mixture into beaten egg yolks in small bowl. Pour egg mixture back into saucepan; cook and stir over low heat until thickened. Remove from heat; stir in vanilla.

4. Spoon half of egg yolk mixture over each chocolate; stir until chocolates are completely melted.

5. Alternate layers of puddings in four parfait glasses. Cover and refrigerate until chilled.

Cakes & Puddings

BERRY BUNDT CAKE

Makes 12 servings

- **4 cups all-purpose flour**
- **2 tablespoons baking powder**
- **2 teaspoons baking soda**
- **1 teaspoon salt**
- **2 cups sugar**
- **1½ cups buttermilk***
- **4 eggs**
- **½ cup vegetable oil**
- **1 teaspoon vanilla**
- **2 cups frozen raspberries**
- **2 cups frozen blueberries**

If you don't have buttermilk, substitute 2¼ teaspoons vinegar or lemon juice plus enough milk to equal ¾ cup. Let stand 5 minutes.

1. Preheat oven to 350°F. Generously grease 12-cup bundt pan.

2. Combine flour, baking powder, baking soda and salt in large bowl; mix well. Whisk sugar, buttermilk, eggs, oil and vanilla in medium bowl until well blended. Add sugar mixture to flour mixture; stir just until dry ingredients are moistened. Fold in raspberries and blueberries. Pour into prepared pan.

3. Bake 1 hour or until toothpick inserted near center comes out clean. Cool in pan on wire rack 20 minutes. Invert onto serving plate.

Cakes & Puddings

DATE GINGERBREAD
Makes 8 servings

1¼ cups plus 1 teaspoon all-purpose flour, divided

¾ cup finely chopped pitted dates (about 18 whole dates)

½ cup whole wheat flour

¼ cup packed brown sugar

1 tablespoon finely chopped candied ginger

½ teaspoon baking powder

½ teaspoon baking soda

½ teaspoon ground ginger

½ teaspoon ground nutmeg

½ teaspoon salt

½ cup water

½ cup molasses

¼ cup canola or vegetable oil

2 eggs

Sweetened whipped cream (recipe follows, optional)

1. Preheat oven to 350°F. Grease 8-inch round cake pan; dust with 1 teaspoon all-purpose flour.

2. Combine remaining 1¼ cups all-purpose flour, dates, whole wheat flour, brown sugar, candied ginger, baking powder, baking soda, ground ginger, nutmeg and salt in large bowl. Add water, molasses, oil and eggs; beat with electric mixer at low speed until combined. Beat at high speed 2 minutes. Pour into prepared pan.

3. Bake 38 to 40 minutes or until toothpick inserted into center comes out clean. Cool in pan on wire rack 10 minutes.

4. Meanwhile, prepare sweetened whipped cream, if desired. Cut cake into wedges; serve warm with whipped cream.

SWEETENED WHIPPED CREAM: Beat 1 cup cold whipping cream and ¼ cup powdered sugar in large bowl with electric mixer at high speed about 1½ minutes or until stiff peaks form.

Cakes & Puddings

TRADITIONAL FRUIT CAKE

Makes 1 loaf

3 cups walnut halves

1 package (8 ounces) candied cherries

1 package (8 ounces) chopped dates

1 package (4 ounces) candied pineapple

3/4 cup sifted all-purpose flour

3/4 cup sugar

1/2 teaspoon baking powder

1/2 teaspoon salt

3 eggs, beaten

3 tablespoons rum extract

1 tablespoon grated orange peel

1 teaspoon vanilla

1. Preheat oven to 300°F. Line 9×5-inch loaf pan with parchment paper; grease paper.

2. Combine walnuts and fruit in large bowl. Combine flour, sugar, baking powder and salt in medium bowl. Sift into walnut mixture; toss gently to coat. Stir in eggs, rum, orange peel and vanilla. Spread batter in prepared pan.

3. Bake 1 hour 45 minutes or until golden brown. Cool completely in pan on wire rack. Remove from pan using parchment; cut into thin slices.

Cakes & Puddings

CARAMELIZED SUGAR CAKE

Makes 10 to 12 servings

1½ **cups sugar, divided**

½ **cup boiling water**

2 **eggs, separated**

2¼ **cups all-purpose flour**

1 **tablespoon baking powder**

1 **teaspoon salt**

½ **cup (1 stick) butter,
softened**

½ **teaspoon vanilla**

½ **teaspoon almond extract**

1 **cup milk**

**Caramel Frosting
(page 153)**

1. Heat ½ cup sugar in small heavy saucepan over medium heat without stirring until sugar is melted and golden brown. Reduce heat to low. Gradually stir boiling water into sugar mixture; cook and stir until sugar is dissolved. Remove from heat.

2. Preheat oven to 375°F. Grease and flour two 8-inch round cake pans.

3. Beat egg whites in large bowl with electric mixer at medium-high speed until foamy. Gradually add ½ cup sugar, beating at high speed until stiff peaks form. Transfer to medium bowl. Combine flour, baking powder and salt in small bowl.

4. Beat butter and remaining ½ cup sugar in same large bowl with electric mixer at medium-high speed until light and fluffy. Beat in egg yolks, vanilla and almond extract. Gradually add sugar syrup, mixing until well blended. Add dry ingredients alternately with milk, beating well after each addition. Fold in egg white mixture. Pour batter into prepared pans.

5. Bake 20 to 25 minutes or until toothpick inserted into centers comes out clean. Cool in pans on wire racks 10 minutes. Remove to wire racks; cool completely.

6. Prepare Caramel Frosting.

7. Place one cake layer on plate. Spread with about 1 cup frosting. Top with second layer. Frost top and side with remaining frosting.

Cakes & Puddings

CARAMEL FROSTING: Melt 2 tablespoons butter in medium saucepan over medium heat. Stir in $2/3$ cup packed brown sugar, $1/3$ cup evaporated milk and $1/8$ teaspoon salt. Bring to a boil, stirring constantly. Remove from heat; cool slightly. Stir in 1 teaspoon vanilla. Beat in $2\frac{1}{2}$ cups powdered sugar until frosting is of spreading consistency.

PEANUT BUTTER PUDDING

Makes 6 servings

2 cups milk

2 eggs

⅓ cup creamy peanut butter

¼ cup packed brown sugar

¼ teaspoon vanilla

Shaved chocolate (optional)

1. Preheat oven to 350°F. Grease six 3-ounce ovenproof custard cups.

2. Combine milk, eggs, peanut butter, brown sugar and vanilla in blender; blend at high 1 minute. Pour into prepared custard cups. Place cups in 13×9-inch baking pan; carefully add enough hot water to baking pan to come halfway up sides of custard cups.

3. Bake 50 minutes or until pudding is set. Remove custard cups from pan; cool to room temperature. Refrigerate until ready to serve.

4. Just before serving, top each pudding with shaved chocolate, if desired.

Cakes & Puddings

APPLE CAKE

Makes 16 to 24 servings

4 medium apples, peeled and cut into ¼-inch slices (4 cups)

Juice of ½ lemon

1 cup plus 1 tablespoon sugar, divided

3 cups all-purpose flour

¾ cup chopped almonds

1½ teaspoons baking soda

1 teaspoon ground cinnamon

½ teaspoon salt

½ teaspoon ground nutmeg

1 cup vegetable oil

1 teaspoon vanilla

1. Preheat oven to 350°F. Grease 13×9-inch baking pan.

2. Place apples in medium bowl. Drizzle with lemon juice and sprinkle with 1 tablespoon sugar; toss to coat. Let stand 20 minutes or until juice forms.

3. Combine flour, remaining 1 cup sugar, almonds, baking soda, cinnamon, salt and nutmeg in large bowl; mix well. Add oil and vanilla; stir until well blended. Stir in apple mixture. Spread batter in prepared pan.

4. Bake about 35 minutes or until top is browned and toothpick inserted into center comes out clean. Cool in pan on wire rack 10 minutes. Serve warm.

Cakes & Puddings

CLASSIC CHOCOLATE BUTTERMILK CAKE

Makes 10 to 12 servings

2 cups all-purpose flour

3¼ cups sugar, divided

⅔ cup unsweetened cocoa powder

2 teaspoons baking soda

1½ teaspoons baking powder

¾ teaspoon salt

1¾ cups buttermilk

½ cup vegetable oil

2 eggs

2 teaspoons vanilla, divided

6 ounces unsweetened chocolate, chopped

½ cup (1 stick) butter, cut into ¼-inch pieces

1 cup whipping cream

1. Preheat oven to 350°F. Line bottoms of two 9-inch cake pans with parchment paper; grease paper.

2. Combine flour, 1¾ cups sugar, cocoa, baking soda, baking powder and salt in large bowl. Whisk buttermilk, oil, eggs and 1 teaspoon vanilla in medium bowl until well blended. Stir into flour mixture until well blended. Divide batter between prepared pans.

3. Bake 22 to 24 minutes or until toothpick inserted into centers comes out clean. Cool in pans 10 minutes. Remove to wire racks; cool completely.

4. For glaze, place chocolate and butter in medium bowl. Heat remaining 1½ cups sugar and cream in small saucepan over medium-high heat, stirring until sugar is dissolved. When cream begins to bubble, reduce heat and simmer 5 minutes. Pour over chocolate; stir until smooth. Stir in remaining 1 teaspoon vanilla. Refrigerate until frosting is cool and thickened, stirring occasionally.

5. Place one cake layer on serving plate; spread with 1 cup frosting. Top with second cake layer; frost top and side of cake with remaining frosting. Refrigerate at least 1 hour before slicing. Refrigerate leftovers.

Cakes & Puddings

PIES & FRUIT DESSERTS

BERRY CRUMBLE BARS
Makes 12 to 16 servings

3 cups all-purpose flour

¹/₂ cup plus ¹/₃ cup granulated sugar, divided

¹/₂ cup packed brown sugar

1 teaspoon baking powder

1 teaspoon grated lemon peel

¹/₂ teaspoon salt

1 cup (2 sticks) cold butter, cut into ¹/₄-inch pieces

1 egg, beaten

2¹/₂ tablespoons lemon juice

1 tablespoon cornstarch

1 package (16 ounces) frozen mixed berries (do not thaw)

Vanilla ice cream (optional)

1. Preheat oven to 375°F. Grease 9-inch square baking pan or line with parchment paper.

2. Combine flour, ¹/₂ cup granulated sugar, brown sugar, baking powder, lemon peel and salt in large bowl; mix well. Add butter and egg; mix with pastry blender or fingertips until a crumbly dough forms. Pat one third of dough into prepared pan.

3. Combine remaining ¹/₃ cup granulated sugar, lemon juice and cornstarch in medium bowl; mix well. Add berries, stir gently until well blended and berries are completely coated with sugar mixture. Spread evenly over crust. Top with remaining dough, crumbling into large pieces over fruit.

4. Bake 45 to 50 minutes or until top is golden brown. Cool in pan on wire rack. (Refrigerating bars for several hours will make them easier to cut.) Serve with ice cream, if desired.

MIXED BERRY SKILLET PIE
Makes 8 servings

Single-Crust Pie Pastry (recipe follows)

2 **packages (12 ounces each) frozen mixed berries**

⅓ **cup sugar**

3 **tablespoons cornstarch**

2 **teaspoons grated orange peel**

¼ **teaspoon ground ginger**

1. Prepare pie pastry.
2. Preheat oven to 350°F.
3. Combine berries, sugar, cornstarch, orange peel and ginger in large bowl; toss gently to coat. Spoon evenly into large cast iron skillet. Roll out pastry to 12-inch circle. Place over skillet; trim and flute edge as desired. Cut several slits in pastry to allow steam to escape.
4. Bake 1 hour or until crust is golden brown. Let stand 1 hour before slicing and serving.

SINGLE-CRUST PIE PASTRY

1¼ **cups all-purpose flour**

½ **teaspoon salt**

6 **tablespoons cold butter, cut into ¼-inch pieces**

3 **to 4 tablespoons ice water**

1½ **teaspoons cider vinegar**

1. Combine flour and salt in medium bowl. Cut in butter with pastry blender or fingertips until mixture resembles coarse crumbs.
2. Combine 3 tablespoons ice water and vinegar in small bowl. Sprinkle over flour mixture, mixing with fork until dough forms. Add additional water as needed.
3. Shape dough into a disc; wrap in plastic wrap. Refrigerate at least 30 minutes.

BAKED ALASKA
APPLE BUTTER PIE
Makes 8 servings

**Single-Crust Pie Pastry
(page 162)**

1 **pint butter pecan ice
cream, softened**

2 **cups apple butter**

1 **can (12 ounces) evaporated
milk**

3 **egg yolks, beaten**

¼ **cup plus 6 tablespoons
packed brown sugar,
divided**

3 **egg whites**

¼ **teaspoon cream of tartar**

½ **teaspoon vanilla**

1. Prepare pie pastry. Roll out into 11-inch circle on lightly floured surface. Line 9-inch pie plate with pastry; trim and flute edge. Refrigerate until ready to fill.

2. Line 8-inch pie plate with plastic wrap. Spread ice cream in prepared pie plate. Cover and freeze until firm.

3. Preheat oven to 425°F. Combine apple butter, evaporated milk, egg yolks and ¼ cup brown sugar in medium bowl. Pour into pie crust.

4. Bake 15 minutes. *Reduce oven temperature to 350°F.* Bake 45 minutes or until knife inserted into center comes out clean. Cool completely on wire rack. Cover and refrigerate at least 1 hour or until ready to serve.

5. Just before serving, preheat oven to 500°F.

6. Beat egg whites and cream of tartar in small bowl with electric mixer at high speed until foamy. Beat in vanilla. Add remaining 6 tablespoons brown sugar, 1 tablespoon at a time, beating until stiff peaks form.

7. Unmold ice cream and invert onto chilled pie. Remove plastic wrap. Spread meringue over ice cream and any exposed surface of pie, covering completely. Bake 2 to 3 minutes or until meringue is golden brown. Serve immediately.

Pies & Fruit Desserts

BUTTERMILK PIE

Makes 8 servings

22 to 24 whole graham crackers*

1½ cups plus ⅓ cup sugar, divided

½ cup (1 stick) butter, melted and cooled, divided

1 tablespoon cornstarch

3 eggs

½ cup buttermilk

1 tablespoon lemon juice

1 teaspoon vanilla

Sweetened whipped cream (page 148, optional)

*Substitute 1½ cups purchased graham cracker crumbs for graham crackers and proceed with step 3.

1. Preheat oven to 350°F.

2. For crust, place crackers in food processor, breaking into smaller pieces if necessary. Process using on/off pulses until finely crushed.

3. Combine cracker crumbs, ⅓ cup sugar and ¼ cup butter in medium bowl; mix well. Press firmly onto bottom and up side of 9-inch pie plate. Bake about 8 minutes or until browned. Cool completely.

4. For filling, combine remaining 1½ cups sugar and cornstarch in large bowl. Beat in eggs, buttermilk, remaining ¼ cup butter, lemon juice and vanilla with electric mixer at medium speed until smooth. Pour into crust.

5. Bake 40 minutes or until set. Cool completely on wire rack. Refrigerate 2 hours or until ready to serve.

6. Prepare sweetened whipped cream, if desired; serve with pie.

Pies & Fruit Desserts

APPLE-PEAR PRALINE PIE

Makes 8 servings

Double-Crust Pie Pastry (page 172)

4 cups sliced peeled Granny Smith apples

2 cups sliced peeled pears

¾ cup granulated sugar

¼ cup plus 1 tablespoon all-purpose flour, divided

4 teaspoons ground cinnamon

¼ teaspoon salt

½ cup (1 stick) plus 2 tablespoons butter, divided

1 cup packed brown sugar

1 tablespoon half-and-half or milk

1 cup chopped pecans

1. Prepare pie pastry.

2. Combine apples, pears, granulated sugar, ¼ cup flour, cinnamon and salt in large bowl; toss to coat. Let stand 15 minutes.

3. Preheat oven to 350°F. Roll out one disc of pastry into 11-inch circle on floured surface. Line deep-dish 9-inch pie plate with pastry; sprinkle with remaining 1 tablespoon flour. Spoon apple and pear mixture into crust; dot with 2 tablespoons butter. Roll out remaining disc of pastry into 10-inch circle. Place over fruit; seal and flute edge. Cut slits in top crust.

4. Bake 1 hour. Meanwhile, combine remaining ½ cup butter, brown sugar and half-and-half in small saucepan; bring to a boil over medium heat, stirring frequently. Boil 2 minutes, stirring constantly. Remove from heat; stir in pecans. Spread over pie.

5. Cool pie on wire rack 15 minutes. Serve warm or at room temperature.

Pies & Fruit Desserts

CINNAMON PLUM WALNUT COBBLER
Makes 9 servings

- ¾ **cup all-purpose flour**
- ½ **cup chopped walnuts**
- ½ **cup plus 3 tablespoons granulated sugar, divided**
- ⅛ **teaspoon salt**
- 6 **tablespoons cold butter, cut into ¼-inch pieces**
- 1 **to 2 tablespoons milk, plus additional for brushing top of dough**
- 8 **red plums (about 2½ pounds), cut into ¼-inch slices**
- 2½ **tablespoons cornstarch**
- ¾ **teaspoon ground cinnamon, divided**
- ½ **cup mascarpone cheese**
- 2 **tablespoons powdered sugar**
- 2 **tablespoons milk**

1. Preheat oven to 350°F. Grease 8-inch square baking dish.

2. Combine flour, walnuts, 1 tablespoon granulated sugar and salt in food processor. Add butter; process until butter is incorporated into mixture. With motor running, add just enough milk through feed tube to form soft dough. Wrap with plastic wrap; refrigerate 30 minutes.

3. Combine plums, ½ cup granulated sugar, cornstarch and ½ teaspoon cinnamon in large bowl; toss to coat. Spread fruit mixture evenly in prepared baking dish.

4. Bake 30 minutes. Meanwhile, roll out dough into 8-inch square. Cut out nine circles with 2¼-inch round cutter. Remove scraps of dough; crumble over baked fruit or discard. Arrange dough circles over fruit; brush lightly with additional milk. Combine remaining 2 tablespoons granulated sugar and ¼ teaspoon cinnamon in small bowl; sprinkle over dough.

5. Bake 30 to 35 minutes or until topping is golden brown. Meanwhile, combine mascarpone, powdered sugar and 2 tablespoons milk in small bowl; whisk until smooth. Serve with warm cobbler.

Pies & Fruit Desserts

DEEP-DISH BLUEBERRY PIE
Makes 8 servings

Double-Crust Pie Pastry (recipe follows)

6 **cups fresh blueberries**

1¼ **cups sugar**

3 **tablespoons quick-cooking tapioca**

2 **tablespoons lemon juice**

¼ **teaspoon ground cinnamon**

1 **tablespoon butter, cut into small pieces**

1. Prepare pie pastry. Preheat oven to 400°F. Roll out one pastry disc into 11-inch circle on floured surface. Line 9-inch pie plate with pastry.

2. Combine blueberries, sugar, tapioca, lemon juice and cinnamon in large bowl; stir gently until blended. Pour blueberry mixture into crust; dot with butter.

3. Roll out remaining pastry disc into 10-inch circle; cut into ½-inch-wide strips. Arrange in lattice design over fruit. Trim and flute edge.

4. Bake 15 minutes. *Reduce oven temperature to 350°F.* Bake 40 minutes or until crust is golden brown. Cool on wire rack 30 minutes.

DOUBLE-CRUST PIE PASTRY

2 **cups all-purpose flour**

1 **tablespoon sugar**

½ **teaspoon salt**

¾ **cup (1½ sticks) cold butter, cut into ¼-inch pieces**

6 **to 8 tablespoons ice water**

1 **tablespoon cider vinegar**

1. Combine flour, sugar and salt in medium bowl. Cut in butter with pastry blender or fingertips until mixture resembles coarse crumbs.

2. Combine 6 tablespoons ice water and vinegar in small bowl. Sprinkle water mixture, 1 tablespoon at a time, over flour mixture, mixing with fork until dough forms. Add additional water, if necessary.

3. Divide dough in half. Shape each half into a disc; wrap in plastic wrap. Refrigerate at least 30 minutes.

Pies & Fruit Desserts

LEMON CHESS PIE
Makes 8 servings

Single-Crust Pie Pastry (page 162)

3 eggs

2 egg yolks

1³/₄ cups sugar

½ cup half-and-half

⅓ cup lemon juice

¼ cup (½ stick) butter, melted

3 tablespoons grated lemon peel

2 tablespoons all-purpose flour

Sweetened whipped cream (page 148, optional)

1. Prepare pie pastry. Roll out into 11-inch circle on lightly floured surface. Line 9-inch pie plate with pastry; trim and flute edge. Refrigerate until ready to fill.

2. Preheat oven to 325°F.

3. Whisk eggs and egg yolks in large bowl. Whisk in sugar, half-and-half, lemon juice, butter, lemon peel and flour until well blended. Pour into crust.

4. Bake 40 minutes or until almost set. Cool completely on wire rack. Refrigerate 2 hours or until ready to serve.

5. Prepare sweetened whipped cream, if desired. Serve with pie.

NOTE: To determine doneness, carefully shake pie. It is done when only the center 2 inches jiggle.

STRAWBERRY RHUBARB PIE

Makes 8 servings

Double-Crust Pie Pastry (page 172)

1½ **cups sugar**

½ **cup cornstarch**

2 **tablespoons quick-cooking tapioca**

1 **tablespoon grated lemon peel**

¼ **teaspoon ground allspice**

4 **cups sliced rhubarb (1-inch pieces)**

3 **cups sliced fresh strawberries**

1 **egg, lightly beaten**

1. Prepare pie pastry. Preheat oven to 425°F. Roll out one pastry disc into 11-inch circle on floured surface. Line 9-inch pie plate with pastry.

2. Combine sugar, cornstarch, tapioca, lemon peel and allspice in large bowl. Add rhubarb and strawberries; toss to coat. Pour into crust.

3. Roll out remaining pastry disc into 10-inch circle; cut into ½-inch-wide strips. Arrange in lattice design over fruit. Seal and flute edge. Brush pastry with beaten egg.

4. Bake 50 minutes or until filling is thick and bubbly and crust is golden brown. Cool on wire rack. Serve warm or at room temperature.

Pies & Fruit Desserts

SHOOFLY PIE
Makes 8 servings

Single-Crust Pie Pastry (page 162)

1 cup all-purpose flour

²/₃ cup packed brown sugar

¼ cup (½ stick) plus 1 tablespoon butter, cut into ¼-inch pieces, divided

3 eggs

½ cup molasses

½ teaspoon baking soda

²/₃ cup hot water

Sweetened whipped cream (page 148, optional)

1. Prepare pie pastry. Roll out into 11-inch circle on lightly floured surface. Line 9-inch pie plate with pastry; trim and flute edge. Refrigerate until ready to fill.

2. Preheat oven to 325°F. Combine flour and brown sugar in medium bowl.

3. For topping, remove ½ cup flour mixture to small bowl. Cut in 1 tablespoon butter with pastry blender or fingertips until mixture resembles coarse crumbs.

4. Melt remaining ¼ cup butter; cool slightly. Whisk eggs, molasses and melted butter in large bowl. Gradually stir in flour mixture until well blended. Stir in baking soda. Gradually stir in hot water until blended. Pour into crust. Sprinkle with topping.

5. Bake 40 minutes or until filling is puffy and set. Cool completely on wire rack.

6. Prepare sweetened whipped cream, if desired. Serve with pie.

Pies & Fruit Desserts

FIG-STRAWBERRY COBBLER WITH CREAM CHEESE DUMPLINGS

Makes 6 to 8 servings

FILLING

1½ **pounds fresh strawberries, hulled and quartered**

1 **pound fresh or thawed frozen figs, stemmed and quartered**

⅓ **cup packed brown sugar**

2 **tablespoons cornstarch**

2 **teaspoons grated lemon peel**

DUMPLINGS

1 **package (8 ounces) Neufchâtel or regular cream cheese, softened**

5 **tablespoons granulated sugar, divided**

½ **cup plus 2 tablespoons milk**

1 **teaspoon vanilla**

1 **cup all-purpose flour**

1 **teaspoon baking powder**

¼ **teaspoon salt**

1. Preheat oven to 350°F. Grease 9-inch round or 8-inch square baking dish.

2. Combine strawberries, figs, brown sugar, cornstarch and lemon peel in medium bowl; toss to coat. Spoon into prepared baking dish.

3. Beat Neufchâtel cheese and 3 tablespoons granulated sugar in large bowl with electric mixer at high speed until light and fluffy. Add milk and vanilla; beat at medium speed until well blended. Combine flour, baking powder and salt in medium bowl; mix well. Add to cream cheese mixture; stir just until moistened. Drop by rounded tablespoonfuls onto fruit mixture; sprinkle with remaining 2 tablespoons granulated sugar.

4. Bake in center of oven 55 to 60 minutes or until filling is thick and bubbly and dumplings are browned. Let stand 30 minutes before serving.

PEACH CHERRY PIE

Makes 8 servings

Single-Crust Pie Pastry (page 162)

³/₄ **cup old-fashioned oats**

¹/₃ **cup all-purpose flour**

¹/₃ **cup packed brown sugar**

1¹/₄ **teaspoons ground cinnamon, divided**

¹/₄ **cup (¹/₂ stick) butter, melted**

³/₄ **cup granulated sugar**

3 **tablespoons quick-cooking tapioca**

1 **teaspoon grated lemon peel**

¹/₈ **teaspoon salt**

4 **cups sliced peeled peaches (about 7 medium)**

2 **cups Bing cherries, pitted**

1 **tablespoon lemon juice**

2 **tablespoons butter, cut into ¹/₄-inch pieces**

Vanilla ice cream (optional)

1. Prepare pie pastry. Roll out into 11-inch circle on lightly floured surface. Line 9-inch pie plate with pastry; trim and flute edge. Refrigerate until ready to fill.

2. Preheat oven to 375°F.

3. For topping, combine oats, flour, brown sugar and ³/₄ teaspoon cinnamon in medium bowl. Stir in melted butter until mixture resembles coarse crumbs.

4. Combine granulated sugar, tapioca, lemon peel, remaining ¹/₂ teaspoon cinnamon and salt in large bowl. Add peaches, cherries and lemon juice; toss to coat. Spread evenly in crust; dot with cold butter. Sprinkle with topping.

5. Bake 40 minutes or until filling is bubbly. Cool on wire rack 15 minutes. Serve warm or at room temperature with ice cream, if desired.

Pies & Fruit Desserts

BEVERAGES

PEACH ICED TEA
Makes 4 servings

4 cups water

3 black tea bags

¼ cup sugar

1 can (about 11 ounces) peach nectar

1 cup frozen peach slices

Ice cubes

1. Bring water to a boil in medium saucepan over high heat. Remove from heat; add tea bags and let steep 5 minutes. Remove tea bags; stir in sugar until dissolved. Cool to room temperature.

2. Stir in peach nectar and peach slices. Refrigerate until cold. Serve over ice.

STRAWBERRY LEMONADE
Makes 5 servings

1 **cup sugar**

3 **cups water, divided**

1 **cup frozen strawberries**

1½ **cups lemon juice**

1. Combine sugar, 1 cup water and strawberries in small saucepan; bring to a boil over high heat. Boil 5 minutes. Remove from heat; cool completely.

2. Pour strawberry mixture into blender; blend until smooth. Strain into pitcher. Stir in lemon juice and remaining 2 cups water until blended. Refrigerate until cold.

WARM CINNAMON FRUIT PUNCH
Makes about 14 servings (about 2½ quarts)

4 **cinnamon sticks**

Juice and peel of 1 orange

1 **teaspoon whole allspice**

½ **teaspoon whole cloves**

1 **cheesecloth bag**

7 **cups water**

1 **can (12 ounces) frozen cranberry-raspberry juice concentrate, thawed**

1 **can (6 ounces) frozen lemonade concentrate, thawed**

2 **cans (5½ ounces each) apricot nectar**

1. Break cinnamon sticks into pieces. Tie cinnamon sticks, orange peel, allspice and cloves in cheesecloth bag.

2. Combine orange juice, water, juice concentrates and apricot nectar in large saucepan; add spice bag. Bring to a simmer over medium heat. Reduce heat to low; cook 30 minutes or until warm and flavors are blended.

3. Remove and discard spice bag before serving.

186

Beverages

STRAWBERRY
LEMONADE

METRIC CONVERSION CHART

VOLUME MEASUREMENTS (dry)

1/8 teaspoon = 0.5 mL
1/4 teaspoon = 1 mL
1/2 teaspoon = 2 mL
3/4 teaspoon = 4 mL
1 teaspoon = 5 mL
1 tablespoon = 15 mL
2 tablespoons = 30 mL
1/4 cup = 60 mL
1/3 cup = 75 mL
1/2 cup = 125 mL
2/3 cup = 150 mL
3/4 cup = 175 mL
1 cup = 250 mL
2 cups = 1 pint = 500 mL
3 cups = 750 mL
4 cups = 1 quart = 1 L

VOLUME MEASUREMENTS (fluid)

1 fluid ounce (2 tablespoons) = 30 mL
4 fluid ounces (1/2 cup) = 125 mL
8 fluid ounces (1 cup) = 250 mL
12 fluid ounces (1 1/2 cups) = 375 mL
16 fluid ounces (2 cups) = 500 mL

WEIGHTS (mass)

1/2 ounce = 15 g
1 ounce = 30 g
3 ounces = 90 g
4 ounces = 120 g
8 ounces = 225 g
10 ounces = 285 g
12 ounces = 360 g
16 ounces = 1 pound = 450 g

DIMENSIONS

1/16 inch = 2 mm
1/8 inch = 3 mm
1/4 inch = 6 mm
1/2 inch = 1.5 cm
3/4 inch = 2 cm
1 inch = 2.5 cm

OVEN TEMPERATURES

250°F = 120°C
275°F = 140°C
300°F = 150°C
325°F = 160°C
350°F = 180°C
375°F = 190°C
400°F = 200°C
425°F = 220°C
450°F = 230°C

BAKING PAN SIZES

Utensil	Size in Inches/Quarts	Metric Volume	Size in Centimeters
Baking or Cake Pan (square or rectangular)	8×8×2	2 L	20×20×5
	9×9×2	2.5 L	23×23×5
	12×8×2	3 L	30×20×5
	13×9×2	3.5 L	33×23×5
Loaf Pan	8×4×3	1.5 L	20×10×7
	9×5×3	2 L	23×13×7
Round Layer Cake Pan	8×1½	1.2 L	20×4
	9×1½	1.5 L	23×4
Pie Plate	8×1¼	750 mL	20×3
	9×1¼	1 L	23×3
Baking Dish or Casserole	1 quart	1 L	—
	1½ quart	1.5 L	—
	2 quart	2 L	—